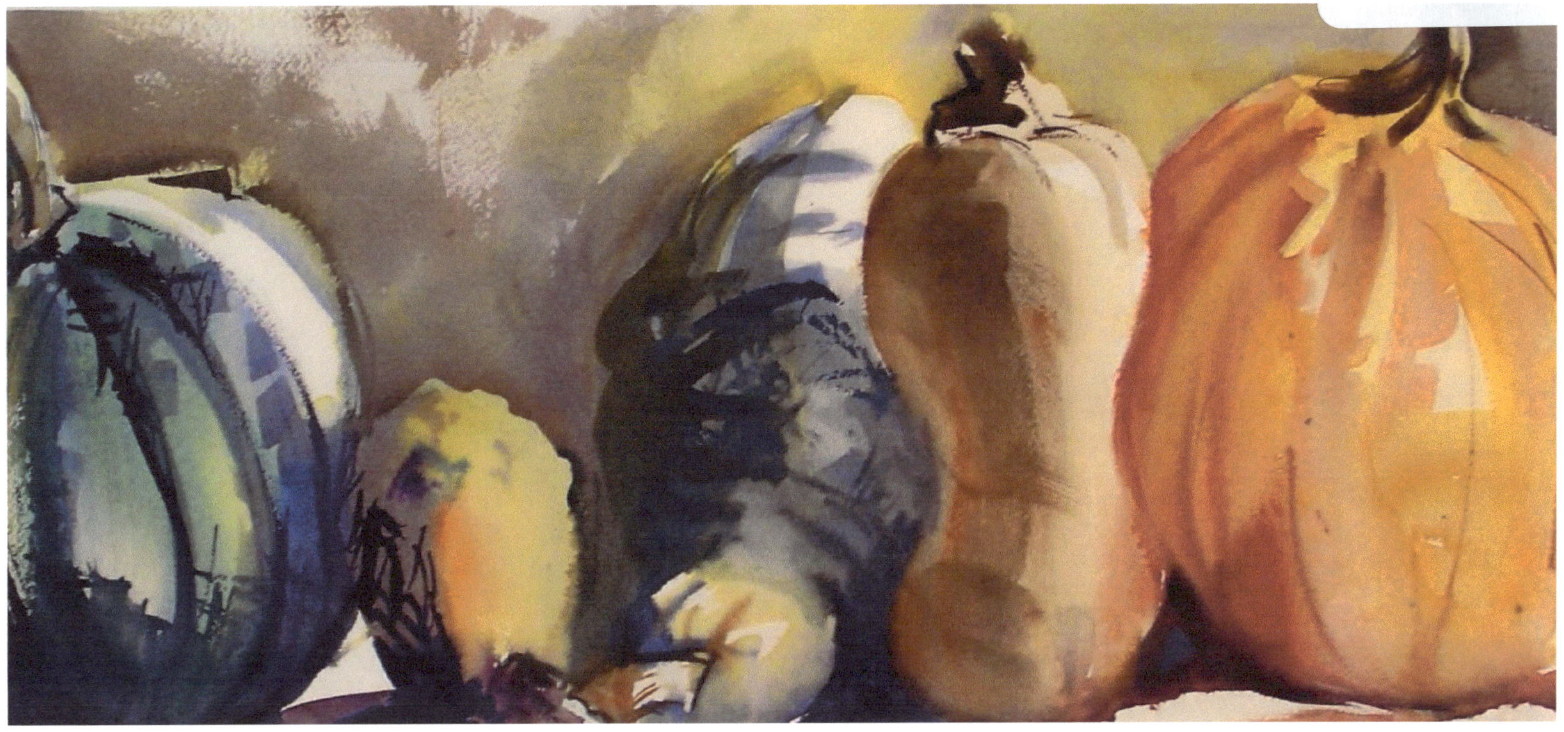

Kitchen Paintings;

watercolors of Alix Hallman Travis

"Awakening" by Carol Little, "Still Life" by Nina Kasanof

"Awakening" by Carol Little, copyright 2011
"Still Life" by Nina Kasanof, copyright 2011

Printed on the occasion of an exhibition,
Kitchen Paintings of Alix Hallman Travis,
at the **Longyear Gallery,** Margaretville, NY,
August 25-September 18, 2011

Cover: **Fall Produc**e, Watercolor, 14x10 in., *private collection*
Title page: **Squashes In a Row**, Watercolor, 21x10 in.

Dedication

Of course, to my husband, Fred, for his enthusiasm and support
and
To my students, both former and present, Carol, Linda, Sumiko and Jane, in whose presence
many of these "Kitchen Paintings" were joyfully painted.

Introduction

When I paint in watercolor my movements and decisions are quick and fluid. I have often thought that my rapid painting strokes were in sync with some kind of internal musical rhythm. As a jazz musician improvises with an instrument on which he is very skilled, I employ my instruments to respond to the subject before me. I make no preliminary drawings, no lightly sketched lines. With my brushes I apply water and pigment to my paper and work to develop shapes inspired by the objects before me. Thirty to forty minutes of intense concentration, attention to an inner voice, constant movement and the painting is accomplished. It may, or may not, bear little resemblance to the actual subject before me.

My practice of painting items from the kitchen began one rainy, frigid day when I could not use my watercolors outside. I wanted to paint and in order to avoid wasting time searching for subject matter I randomly selected some items from my kitchen: fruits, vegetables, containers, whatever caught my fancy. As the cold weather continued so did my raiding the contents of the kitchen. At first this habit was "keeping in practice" and nothing more. Over time painting from the kitchen has grown into an obsession. I am drawn to the shapes and colors found in the kitchen with their unending combinations, much like flavors of a meal, first a fork full of this, then that, maybe a repeat of the second taste, then on to the third--one following another. I share my enthusiasm for this familiar fare with my students, in classes and workshops, and with a growing number of collectors.

As you peruse the images in this book and the paintings hanging on the wall of the exhibition, "Kitchen Paintings" at the **Longyear Gallery,** you will see certain items, like the green plates, my grandmother's knife, or the blue striped tablecloth, appear over and over again. I am comfortable with the familiar, and while these items have been in use in my household for a long time they are seen anew in my paintings. In this way the new merges with the old and they tell the story of my family and my life.

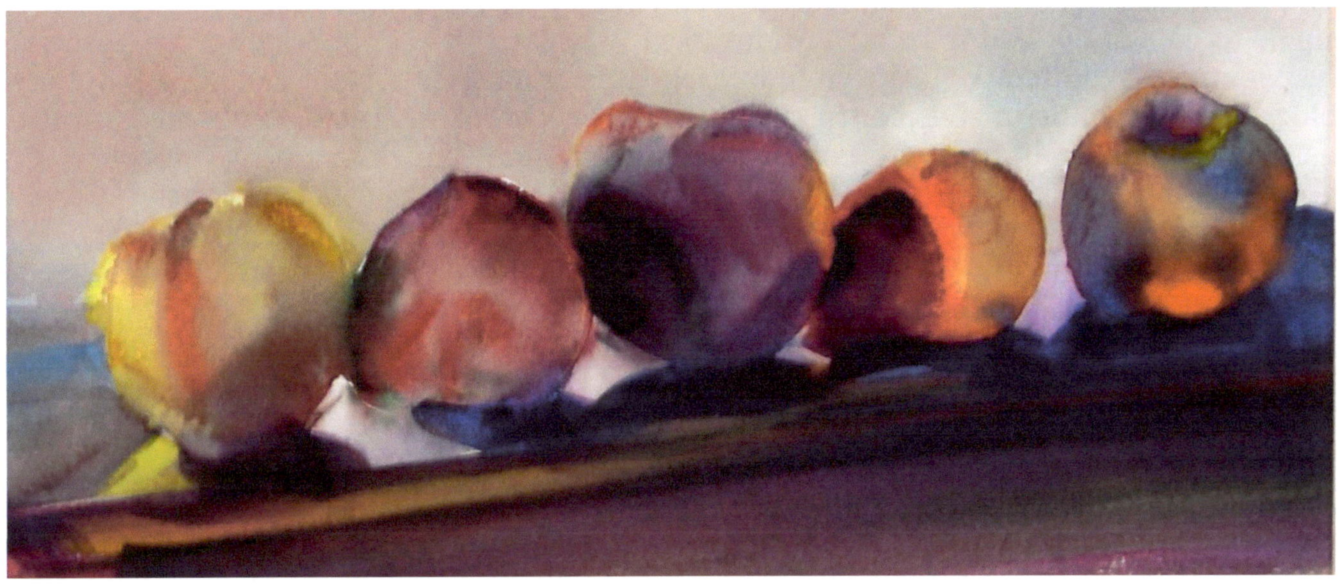

Peaches, no. 1, Watercolor, 14x7 in. *Private collection*

Foreword: Awakening

Alix Travis is my watercolor teacher. She has, like Lonnie Sue Johnson, my first watercolor teacher, entered my life by one of those chance encounters, inspired my creativity, and become my friend. The story of how Alix entered my life must include Lonnie Sue, and how she suddenly left it.

I had been searching for an art class for several years, longing to reconnect with an early passion to draw and paint. I was willing to try almost any class but hoped for a class that at the very least held some appeal to me--and it had to be on a Friday. In the fall of 2004, Cooperstown Art Association offered a Beginning Watercolor class that fit my schedule. I had never been particularly interested in watercolor, but was willing to give it a try. I signed up, walked in, and met Lonnie Sue. I was in the final class of that series, painting with Lonnie Sue on that Friday afternoon in November when my son died.

I continued taking her classes. On December 30, 2007, Lonnie Sue almost died. She was hospitalized suffering from encephalitis. That ended her world as she knew it. As her world changed, so did mine--from life with Lonnie Sue--to life without Lonnie Sue. By then my interest in watercolor was too established to turn back. Once again I searched for a class, this time a watercolor class--and, once again, it had to be on a Friday. I mentioned my search to my friend Jane. She was also interested in finding a teacher.

In September of 2008 Jane and I wanted to canoe on the Delaware River. We decided to try *Al's Sports Store* in Downsville. "Not today," Al stated. "The river is too high." I knew of a place in Halcottsville, *Susan's Pleasant Pheasant Farm*. I knew they rented canoes to those who wanted to paddle on Lake Wawaka. Jane and I drove there and were disheartened to find the place closed-- plenty of canoes sitting near the water but no sign of people or paddles. We glanced around the hamlet that is Halcottsville and decided that we would knock on doors to see if we could find the owners and convince them to rent us a canoe. No responses to our knocks. The final place we came to was an art studio near a large house. We ventured close to the door and could hear voices. We knocked near the open door, peeked in and said "Hello?"

A tall woman with really short white hair motioned us in, stopped mid-sentence, and in one long, enthusiastic breath introduced us to her husband Fred, mentioned his new out-of-town job, and her paintings that he was taking with him. As Fred excused himself, Alix smiled and warmly gestured for us to come all the way in.

She happily showed us around her studio which had once been a blacksmith shop. With great enthusiasm she told us about her paintings hanging amidst the remains of the tools and trappings of the blacksmith. I stared at large brilliant oil paintings of figures dancing, jumping, of buildings, short and tall, of places, near and far. I was amazed by watercolors with splashes of intense color, blotches of dazzling white, soft and hard edged shapes of all kinds--structures, trees, landscapes, figures, interiors--and the paintings that would become part of the grouping she labeled *Kitchen Paintings*. I immediately knew I wanted to learn from her.

Jane and I silently exchanged glances and thoughts. We asked to be her students. Alix immediately said, "I do not teach." Several more times we asked her about taking us on as students. Each time she quickly and adamantly repeated "I do not teach." After about a half hour, saturated with images I would not forget, I joined Jane in expressing thanks, got ready to leave and headed for the door. Alix casually asked, "If I did decide to teach what day could you come?" "Fridays" I blurted. Jane nodded in agreement. "Well," Alix added, "leave your e-mail addresses." Without another word we jotted down our addresses and took our leave, filled with joyful hope. In just a few days we heard from Alix. She had decided she would take us on as students, and laid out the details.

Lonnie Sue now lives in an assisted living facility in Princeton, New Jersey. She has no memory of me. I will not forget how she quietly opened the watercolor door, gently invited me in and made me comfortable, paving the way for Alix, who with strong, steady belief and persistence, pushed me through other doors into rooms of brushstrokes, the darkest of the dark, the lightest of the light, and translucent colors I could not have imagined.

Carol Little
Delhi, NY
June, 2011

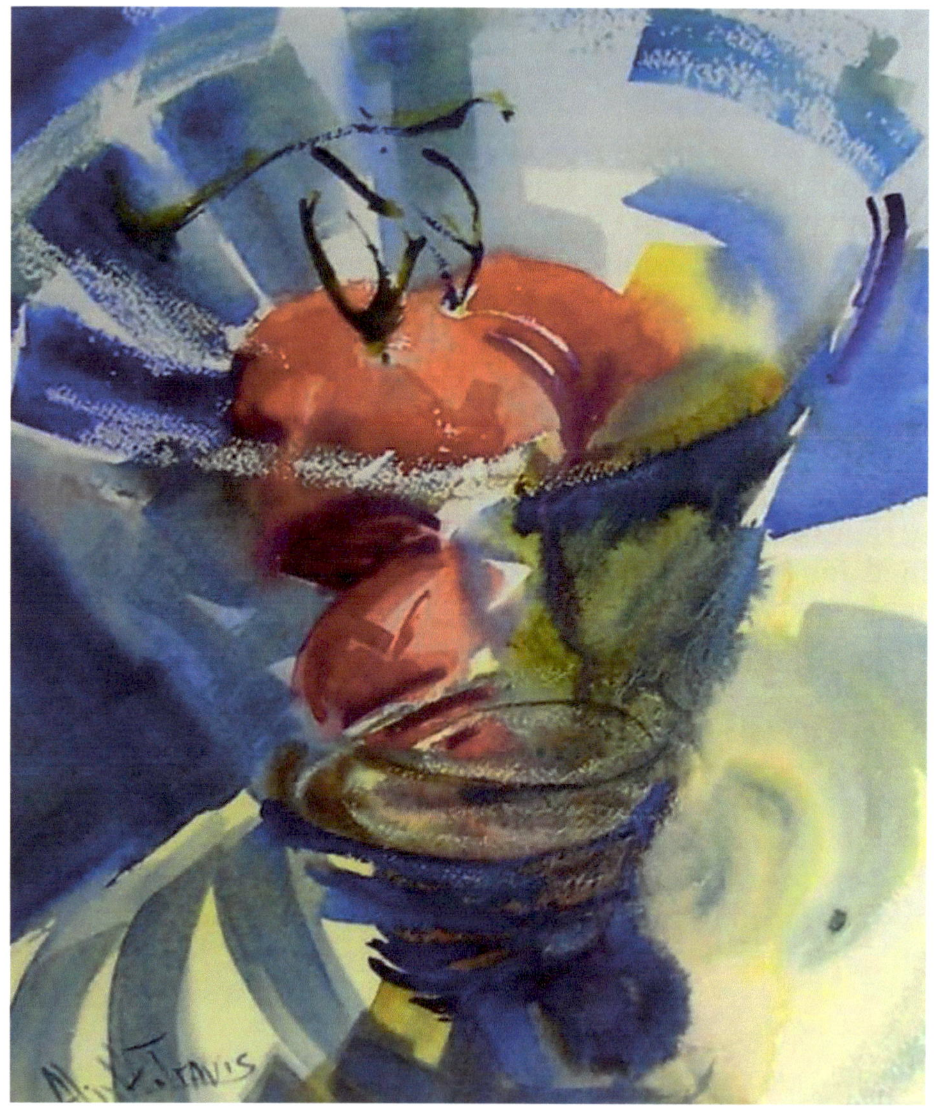

Tomatoes in Bowl, Watercolor, 10x14 in., *private collection*

Still Life

By Nina Kasanof

The Kitchen Paintings of Alix Hallman Travis are still lifes, arrangements of inanimate objects such as fruit, vegetables, and housewares. Although similar subjects appeared far back in ancient art, still life, independent of symbolic meaning, began to play a prominent role in Western painting during the 16th and 17th centuries, with Caravaggio's *Basket of Fruit*, and Spanish artists' depictions of fruit and vegetables set against stark, often dark backgrounds.

But it was the 17th century northern Europe, particularly in the Netherlands and Flanders, that still life became a tremendously popular subject. The term "still life" itself derives from *stilleven*, the Dutch term. In the Netherlands changes were occurring that affected the course of art. The rising middle classes became patrons of the arts, taking over the role that the nobility and the Church played in much of the rest of Europe. The Dutch Protestant Church did not commission large scale religious paintings. It was the private collector who created a demand for art, both as an aesthetic object and as a commodity. Artists could display their works in the open markets, through dealers, or at their studios. Artists tended to specialize in certain subjects, such as portraits, city or seascapes, landscapes, canal scenes, interiors, tavern scenes, and especially popular, still lifes. Some were flower pieces, others were elaborate interiors with oriental rugs covering tables laden with baked goods, meat, fruit, shellfish, glass and metal objects, and sometimes exotic birds. *"Vanitas"* still lifes used objects meant to remind the viewer of the briefness of life and worldly pleasures, employing symbols of transiency such as skulls, mirrors, hourglasses, or dwindling candles. One of the most successful flower painters was Rachel Ruysch, who often included details of beads of water or insects on the petals. Dutch still life painting influenced the art of other countries, and its popularity spread through Europe and America.

Although much of 18th century French painting prior to the Revolution was characterized by a light-hearted frivolous style, the "Rococo," an important exception was Chardin, the leading genre and still life painter of the century. Influenced by Dutch still lifes, he used a restricted range of colors, often earth tones, impasto (thickly applied paint), and layers of color, depicting simple kitchen utensils and objects.

By the late 18th and 19th centuries, still life began to lose its prominence as a subject. Art academies in many European and American cities, dictated certain rules to the artists who wished to become members or exhibit with them. They established certain hierarchies of subjects, placing historical, biblical or mythological subjects as the highest form of painting. Portraits came next, followed by landscape and genre painting, with still life at the bottom of the list. In France, as artistic revolutions occurred throughout the 19th century, still life again became an important subject. Artists such as Delacroix, Courbet and Édouard Manet painted, among a variety of subjects, some wonderful still lifes, and Fantin-Latour was famous for his beautiful flower paintings.

Toward the end of the 19th century, Impressionism and Post-Impressionism brought to still life painting changing approaches to subject matter. Artists such as Monet and Renoir used short, unblended brushstrokes and bright colors to suggest how objects appear to the viewer under changing light conditions. There is no longer any allegorical or mythological content, nor is sharply defined naturalism present. Gauguin used patterns and colors to convey meanings. Van Gogh's *Sunflowers* and *Irises* are some of the most popular of 19th century still lifes. With his thickly-applied paint and rhythmically patterned brushstrokes and heightened color, he even ennobled humble subjects like onions, such as we see in Travis' watercolors.

In America the still life paintings of the Peale family became popular in the early and middle 19th century, often influenced by earlier Dutch painting. The hummingbird and orchid paintings of Martin Johnson Heade showed a variation on traditional still life, and the *trompe-l'oeil* paintings of Harnett and Peto utilized a highly naturalist approach.

At the end of the 19th and beginning of the 20th century in France, we find the Post-Impressionist Cézanne experimenting with the construction of pictorial space, tilting objects and surfaces to suggest changing points of view, as if the spectator were moving about the painting. His still lifes, breaking with traditional rules of perspective, lead directly to Cubism. Picasso and Braque and other Cubists were inspired by late Cézanne compositions, and began to break up and tilt pictorial form and space even further. Still life was an important subject for them, and we find a frequent use of such subjects as wine bottles, grapes, footed fruit dishes, and musical instruments, though they are often so intersected with space in early, or analytical Cubism, that it becomes difficult to separate or interpret the objects. Picasso's and Braque's experiments with collage bought about the second, or synthetic, phase of Cubism, where a greater range of color is used, and objects either suggest pasted elements or are truly pasted in.

Important 20th century still life artists include the Italian painter Morandi, whose simple arrangements of bottles were done almost in monochrome, Redon, the French artist whose vases of flowers seem to exist in a fantasy world, and the American artist, Georgia O'Keeffe, who enlarged and abstracted natural forms such as flowers, animal skulls, and other natural forms.

A new use of still life objects came about in the Pop Art movement of the 1960's and 1970's, which showed objects from popular culture, such as Andy Warhol's soup can paintings, Jasper Johns' American flags and Wayne Thibaud's paintings of cakes and pies. Super Realists also depicted still life objects in a style which rivals the effects of photography.

Today's artists can make choices from a vast range of styles, dictated by their own sensibilities. The Kitchen Paintings of Alix Hallman Travis utilize recognizable and familiar still life objects, but the paintings are less about the objects than about the fluidity of the watercolor medium, the movement of the brushstrokes, and the intensity of color. The viewer can almost participate in the process of making these pictures, and can revel in the finished product.

Nina Kasanof, Ph.D.
Halcott Center, NY
June, 2011

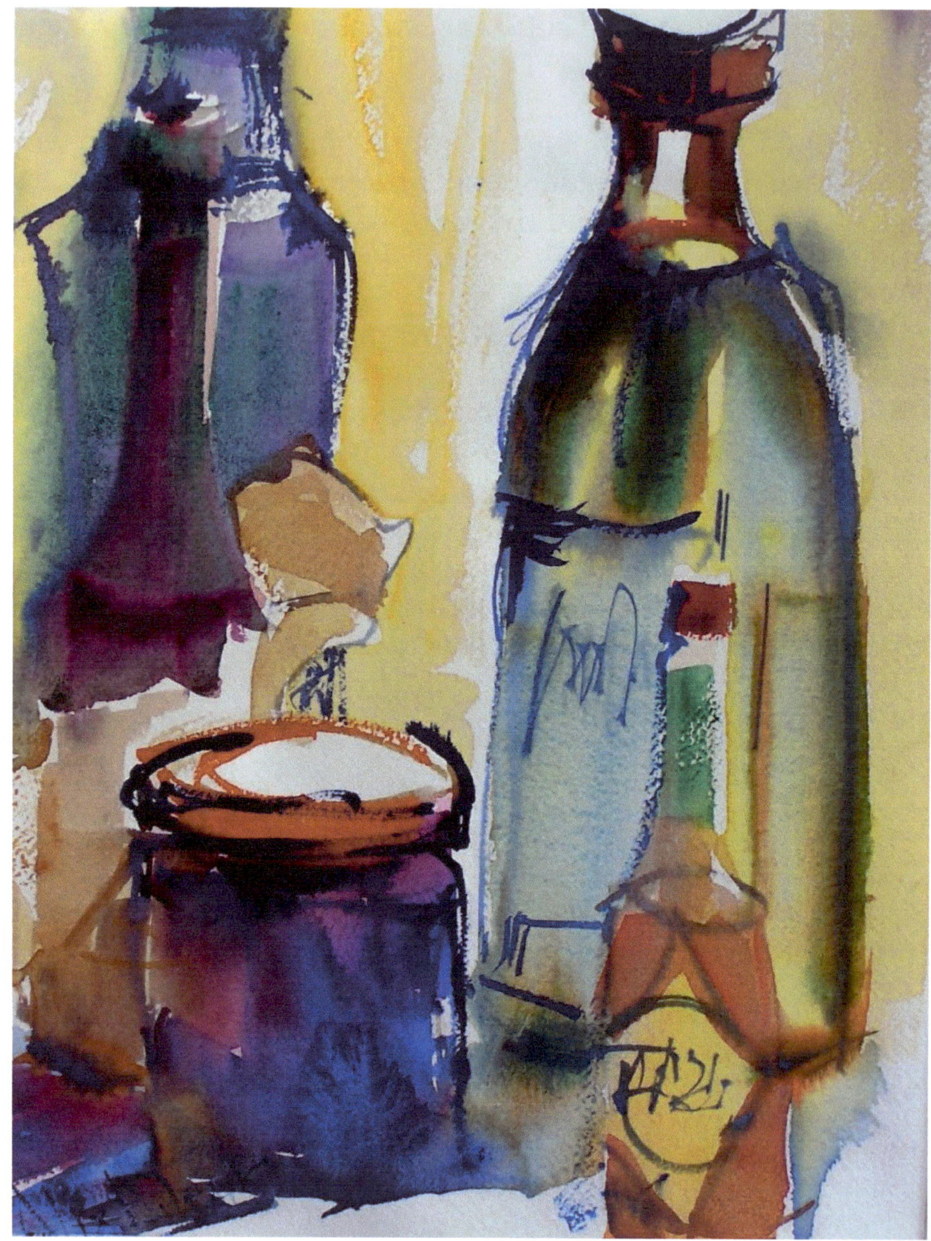

Bottles with Tabasco Sauce, Watercolor, 10x14 in.

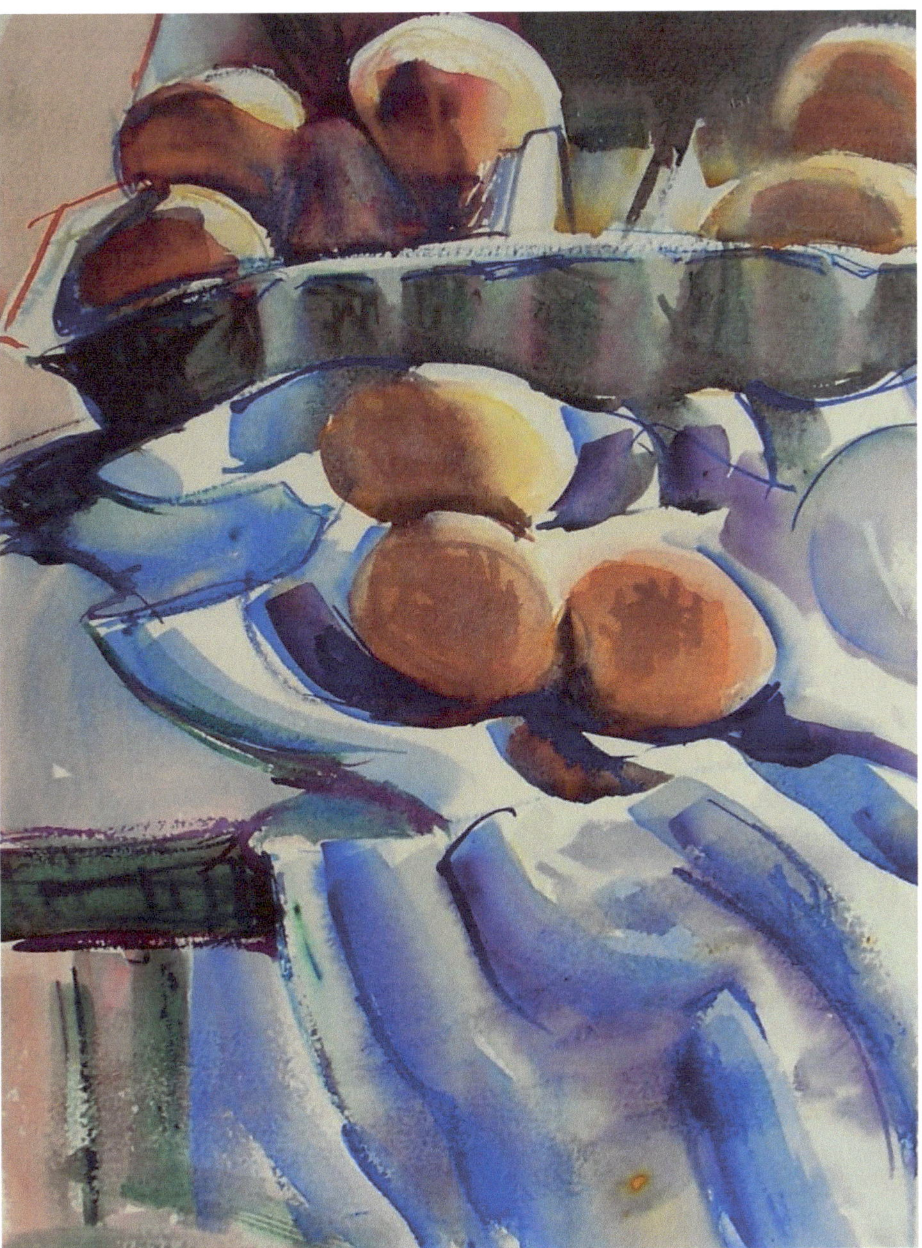

Eggs on Stripes, Watercolor, 10x14 in.

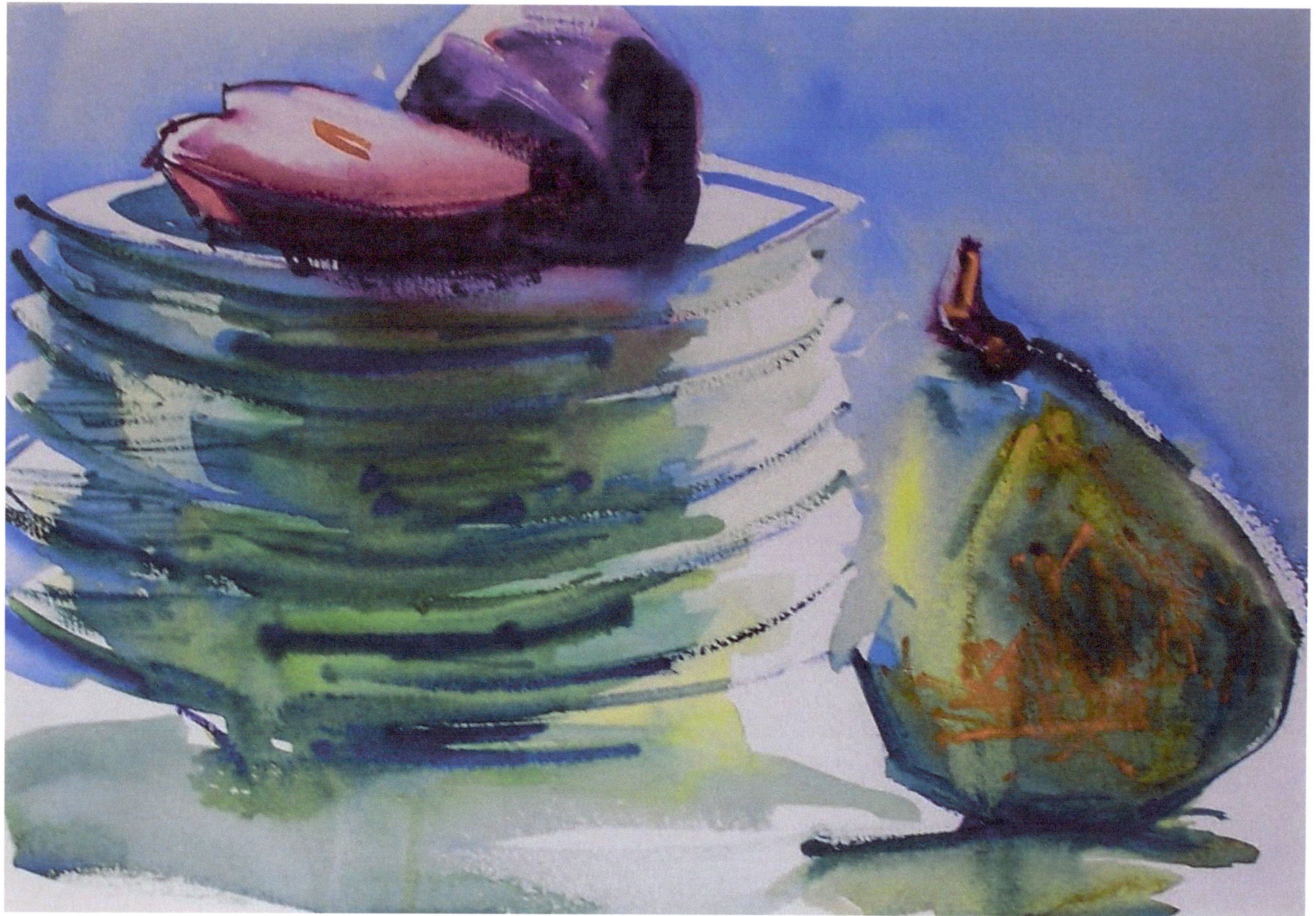

Pears with Green Plates, Watercolor, 14x10 in.

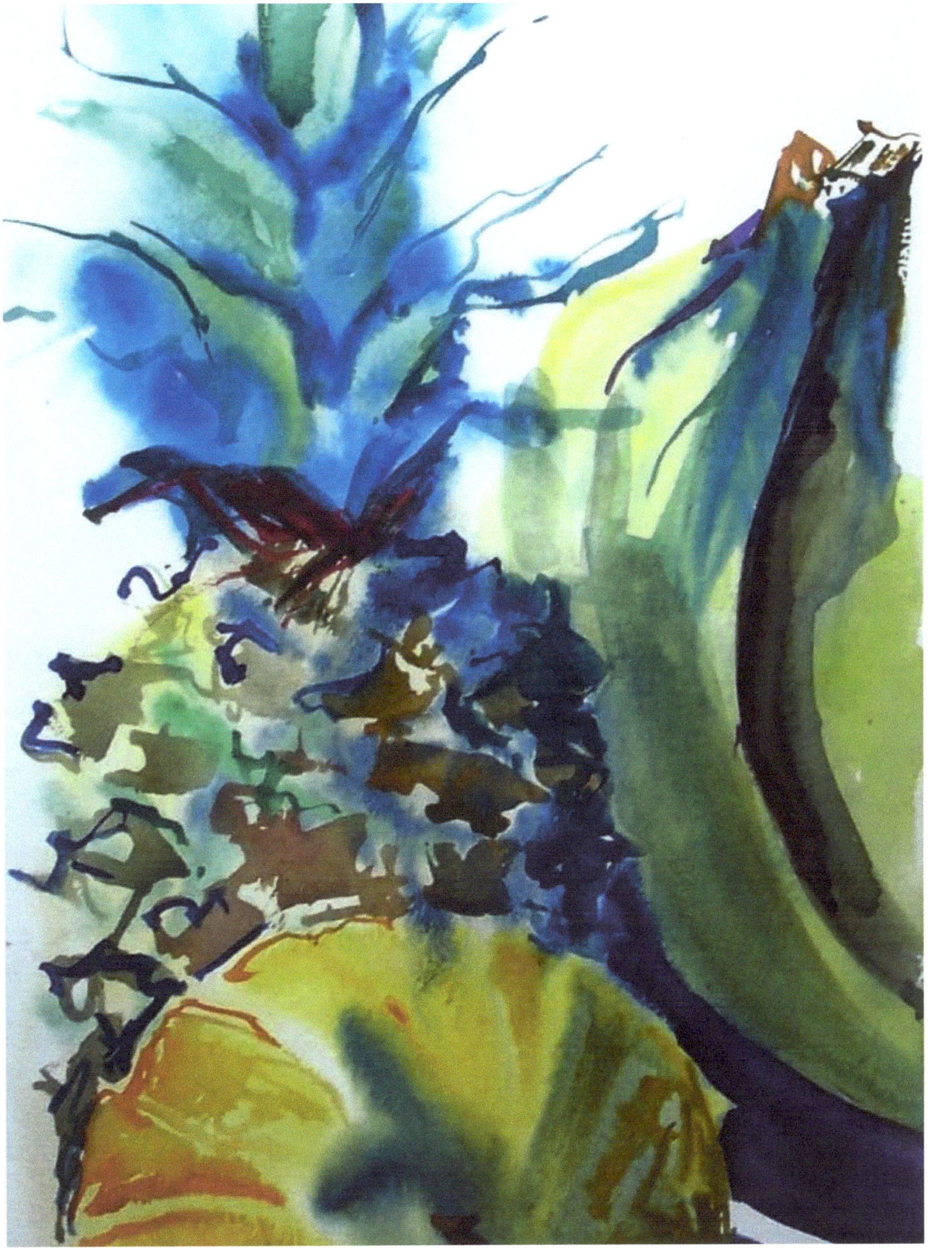

Banana, Pineapple and Galia Melon, Watercolor, 10x14 in.

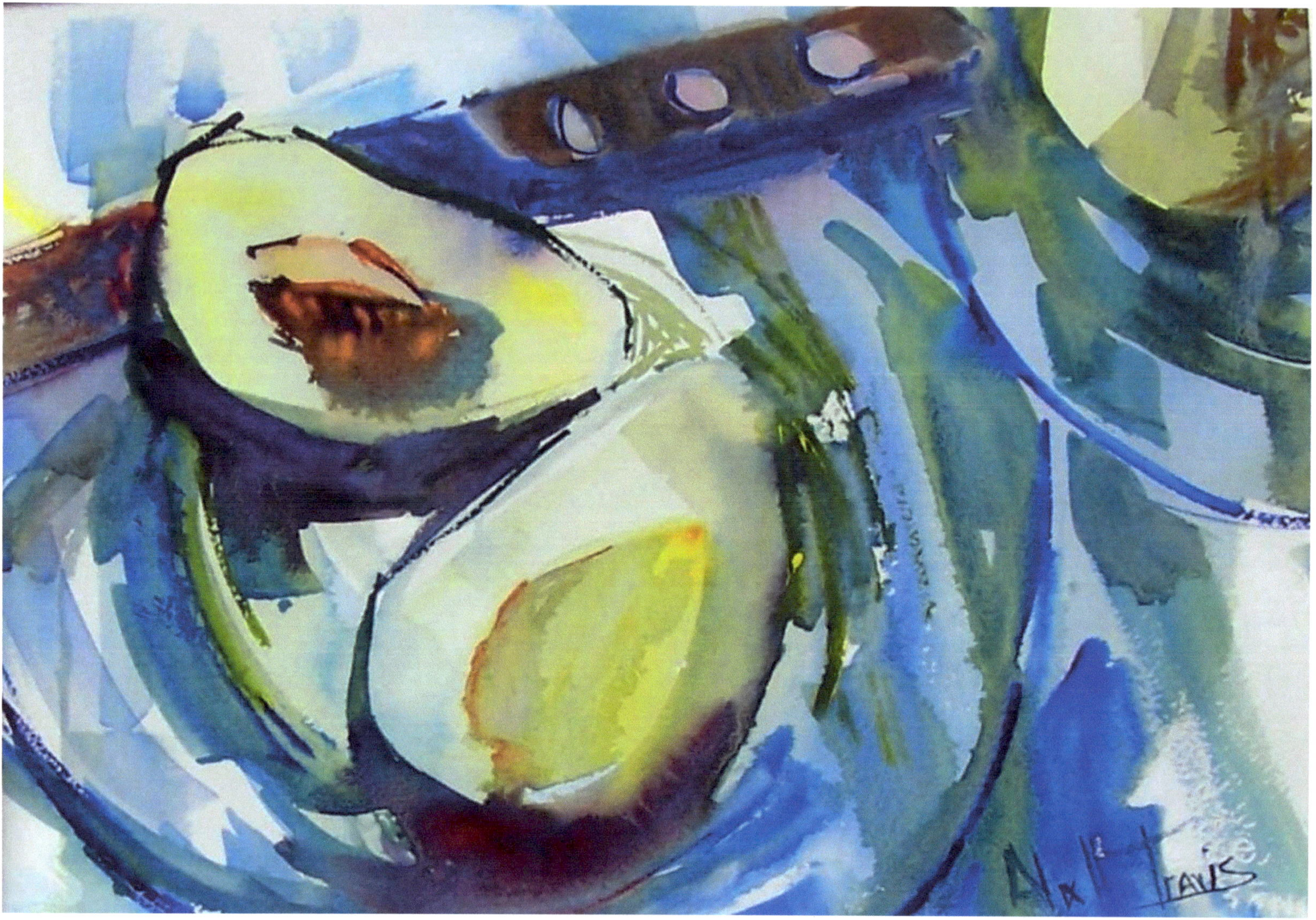

Avocados on Green Plates, Watercolor, 14x10 in.

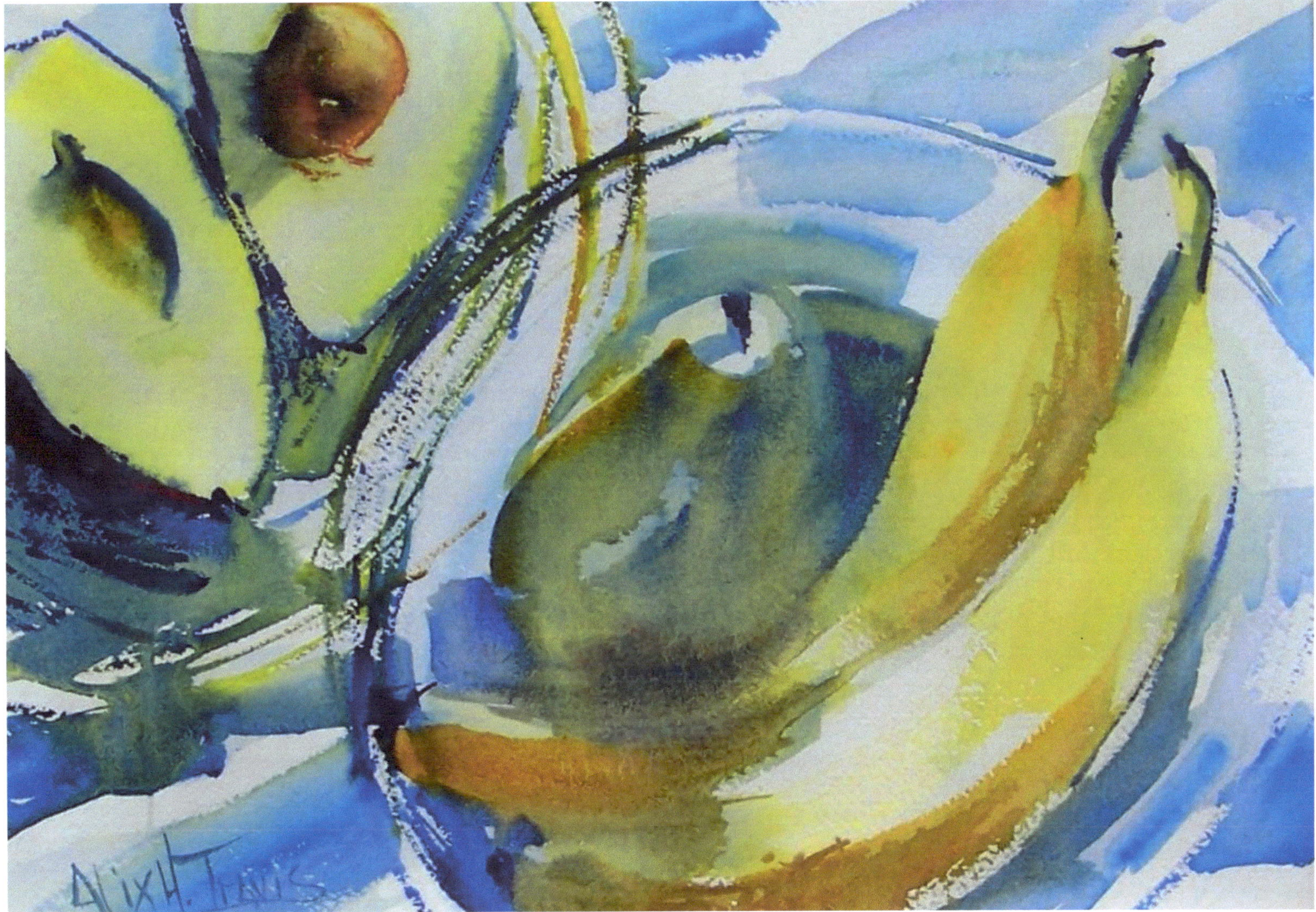

Bananas, Avocado and Pear on Green Plate, Watercolor, 14x10 in.
***"Best of Show"*, Northeast Watercolor Society**, 2010.

Grandmother's Refrigerator Rolls;
also know as **Parker House Rolls** for the famous Boston hotel where they originated

I always prepare Grandmother's rolls when I need real economy of effort; I need a bread with the meal AND a desert. In my childhood home in Tennessee most meals included a hot bread. The dough for these rolls was kept in a bowl under a damp towel in the "ice box" or refrigerator. When my mother, called "Grandmother" by my children, needed rolls for the next meal she would take the bowl from the "ice box", stir the risen dough and let it come to room temperature. About 1 or 1 ½ hours before cooking she built a pile of flour on a board or the counter and spooned a portion of the very wet batter into the flour. Using a knife, spoon or spatular she would press the flour into the dough until she could push it around with her fingers. A couple of light kneads and the wet dough became very elastic. She rolled the kneaded dough to **1**/4 in. thick and cut circles with the open end of a juice glass.

In the meantime, Grandmother would melt ½ stick of butter and a few tablespoons of corn oil in a large, 10 in. iron skillet, and then arrange a spoon under the skillet so that the shortening would collect at one side of the pan. Taking each circle of dough and dipping it into the oil, she would fold it in half and place each snugly at the top of the pan, working to the bottom until the pan was full. (At this point the rolls can be frozen to resume the process later.) She would put the pan full of unbaked rolls aside in a warm place and wait for the them to rise. Just before one would think they would surely fall, she baked them at 400 degrees for about 15-20 min. until browned on top. After baking she often left them in the heavy iron pan where they stayed warm until ready to eat. Any rolls not eaten with the meal became desert with jelly. (Leftover rolls are easily reheated in the microwave for later meals.)

1 package yeast	1 cup scalded milk (I use dry, nonfat milk)
1 teasp sugar	**to the scaled milk add**
½ c lukewarm water	1/3 c melted shortening
Put together in a bowl and allow yeast	1/3 c sugar
to dissolve	2 teasp salt
	1 beaten egg
	flour

Stir several cups of flour into the yeast mixture to make a very wet dough and beat till lumps disappear. Set aside under a warm, wet dishtowel and let rise. Stir risen dough and place in refrigerator until ready to make up as described above. Enjoy!

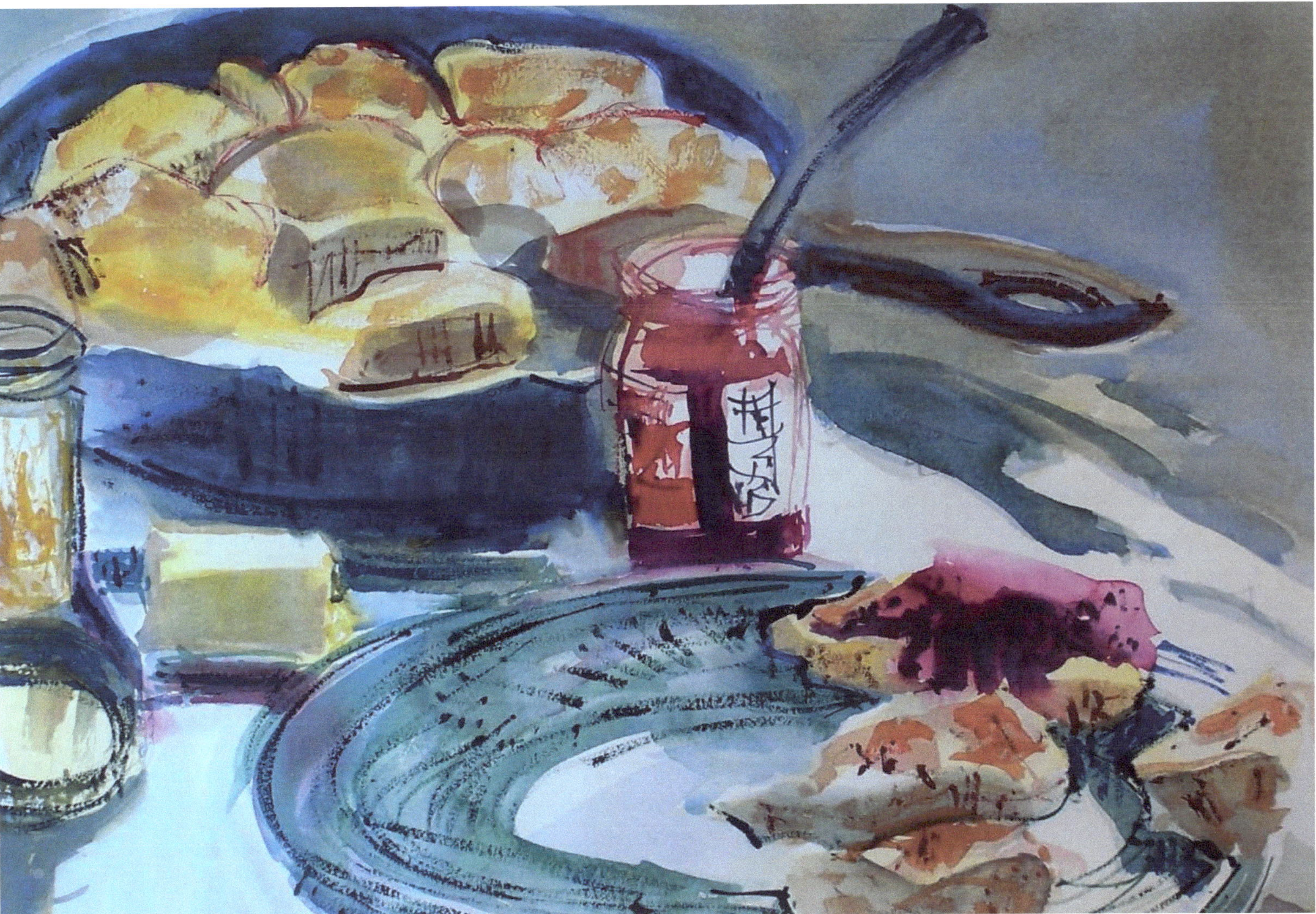

Grandmother's Rolls, Watercolor, 20x14 in.

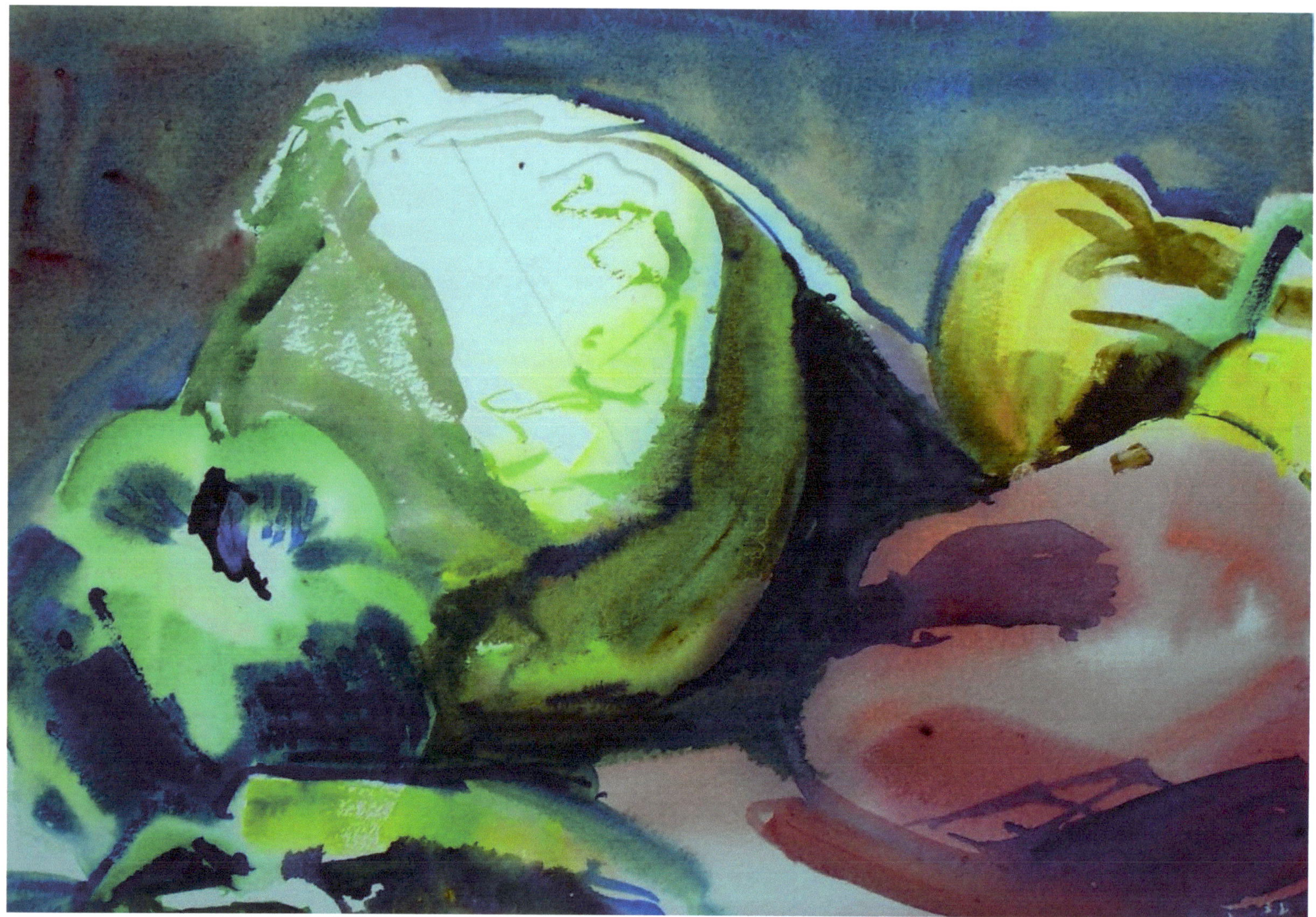

Cabbage with Peppers, Watercolor, 14x10 in.

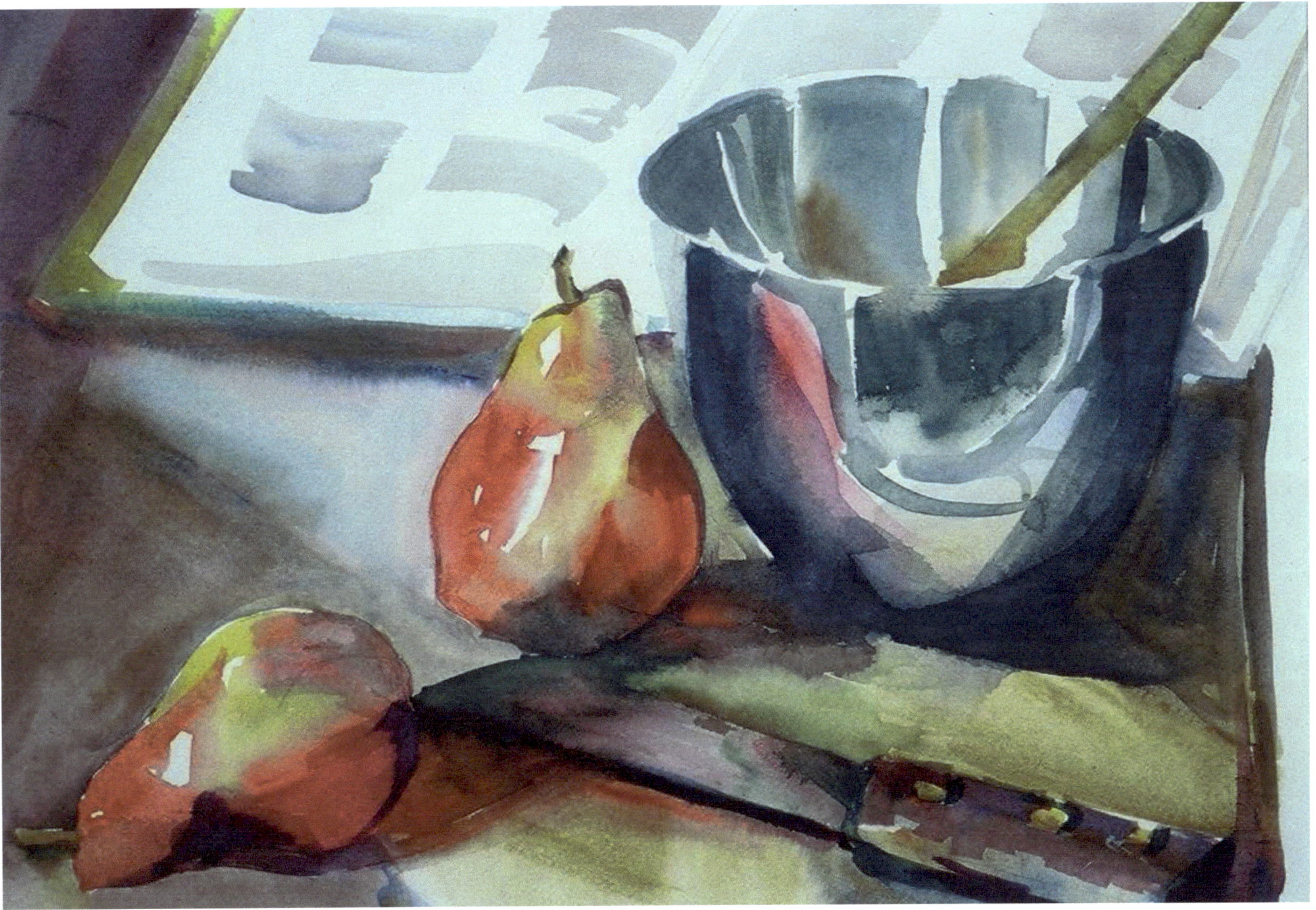

Pear Tart, Watercolor, 16x13.5 in.

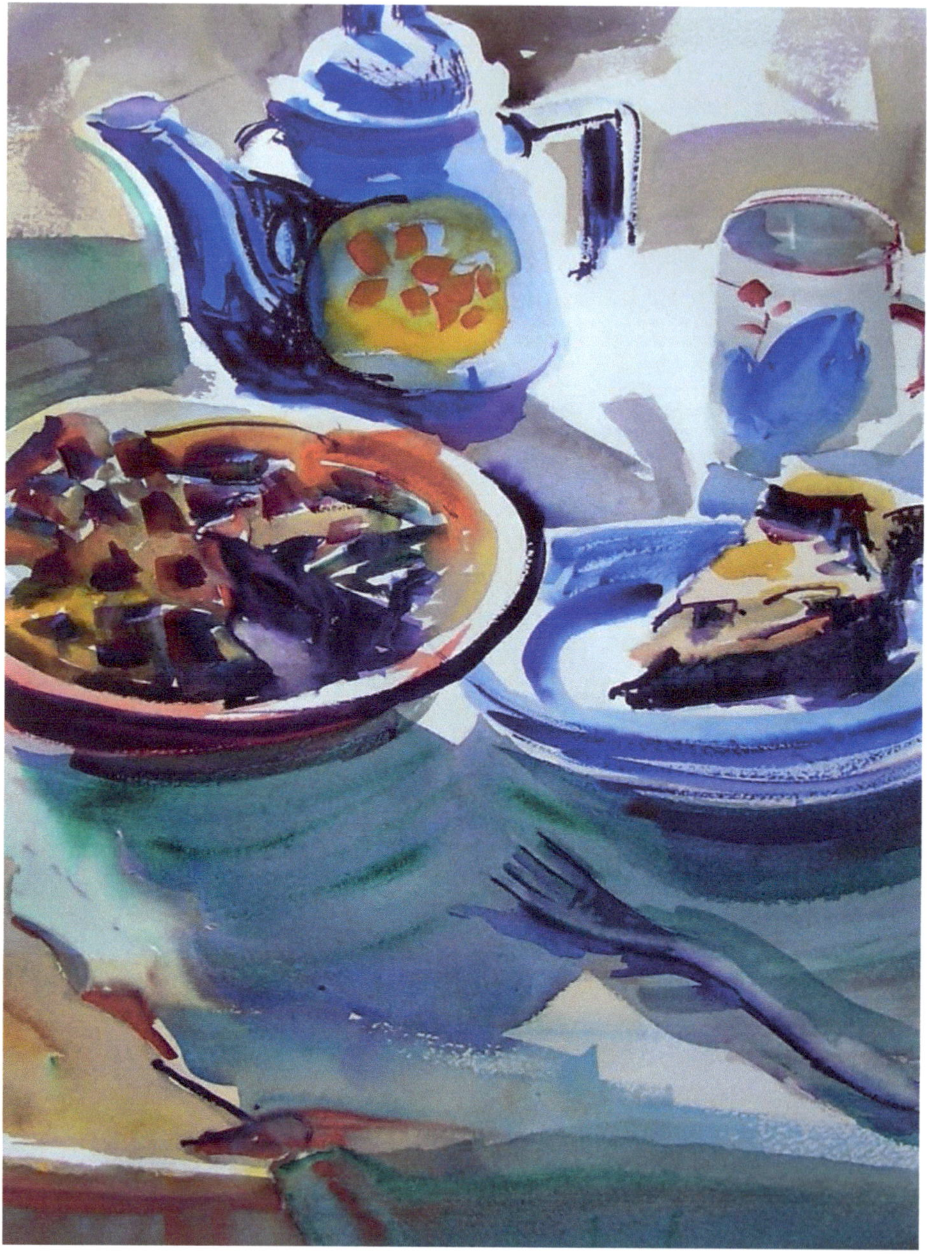

Blueberry Pie with Tea, Watercolor, 14x21 in.

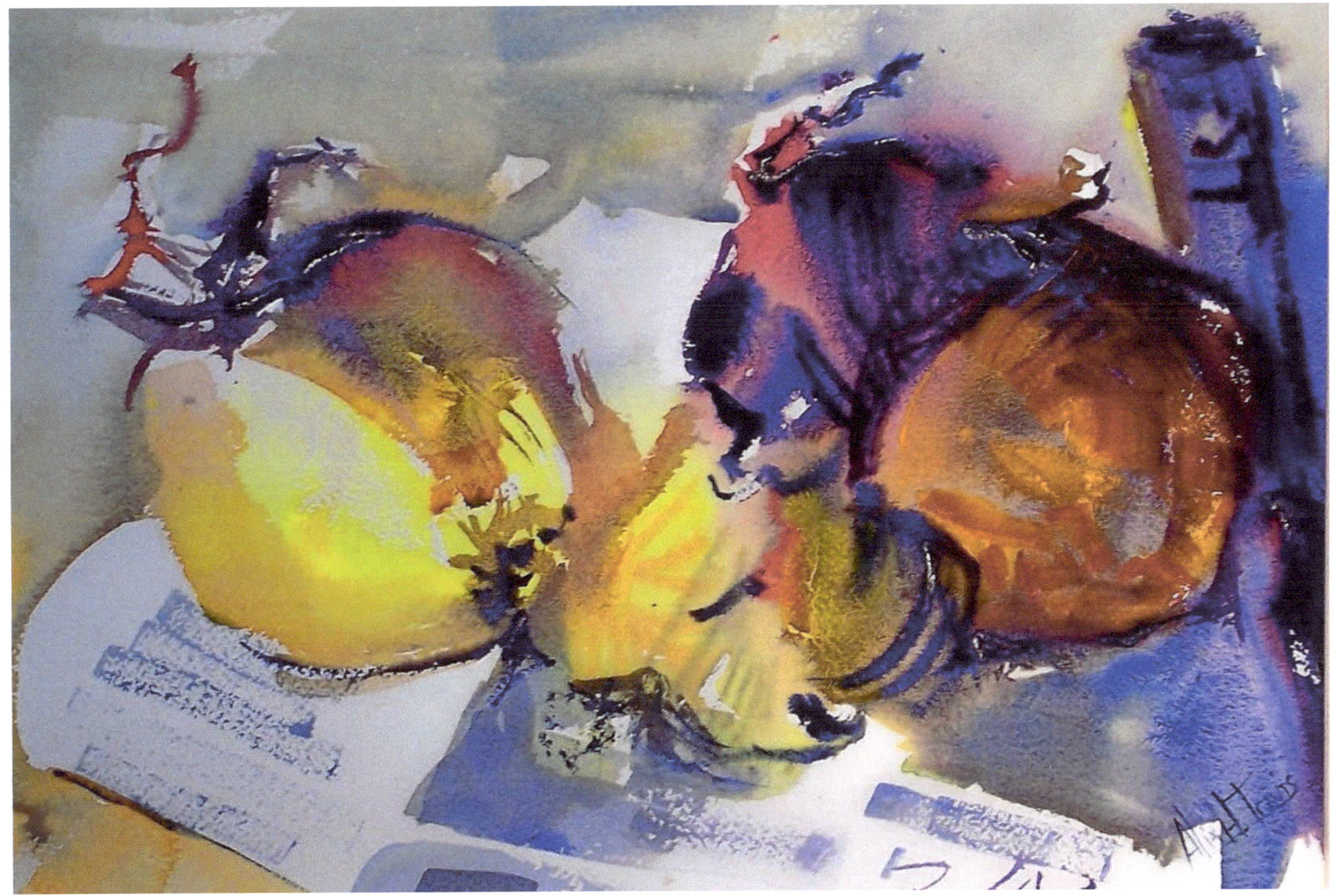

Onions on Newspaper, Watercolor, 14x10 in.

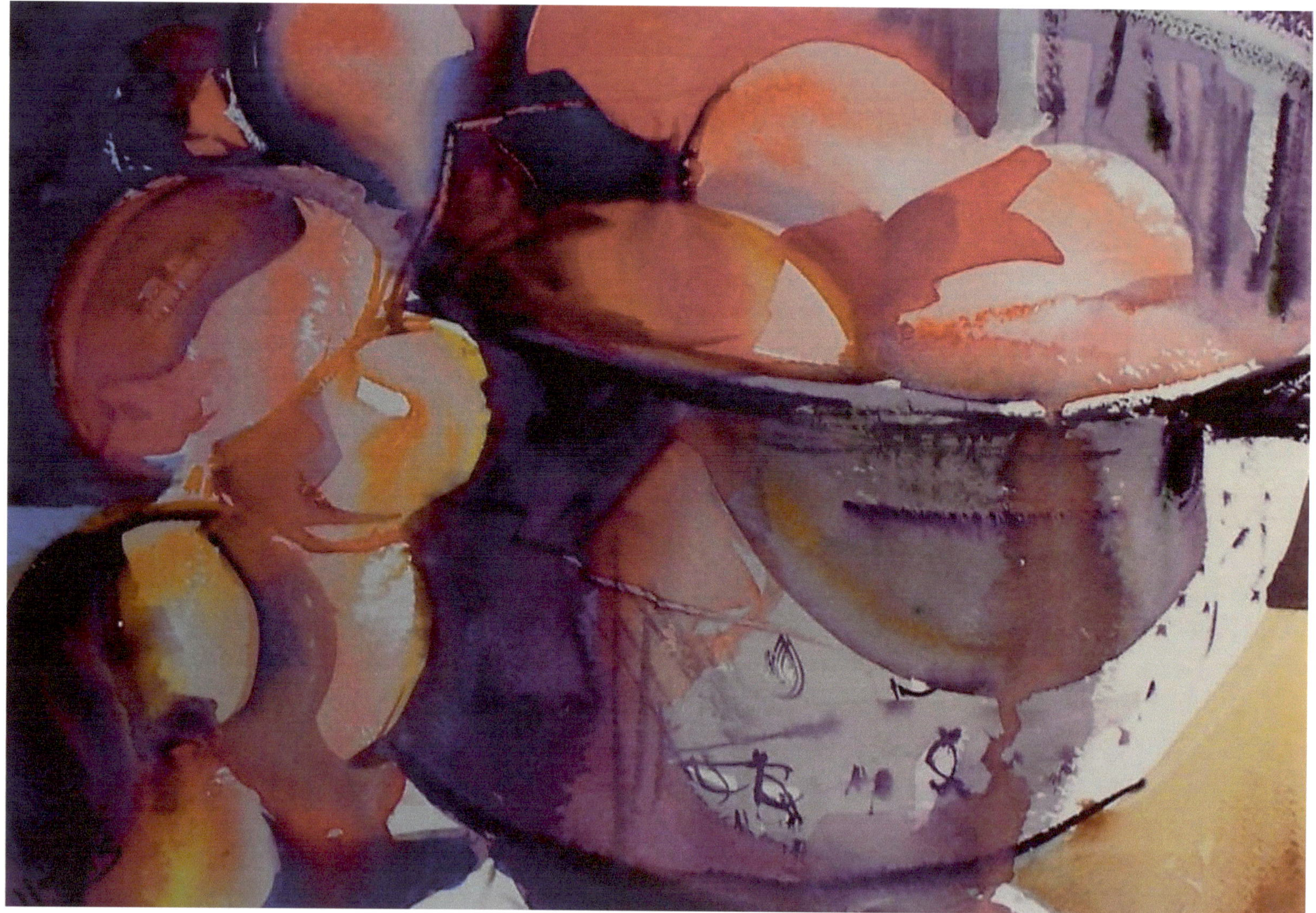

Grapes in Colander,Watercolor, 14x10 in.

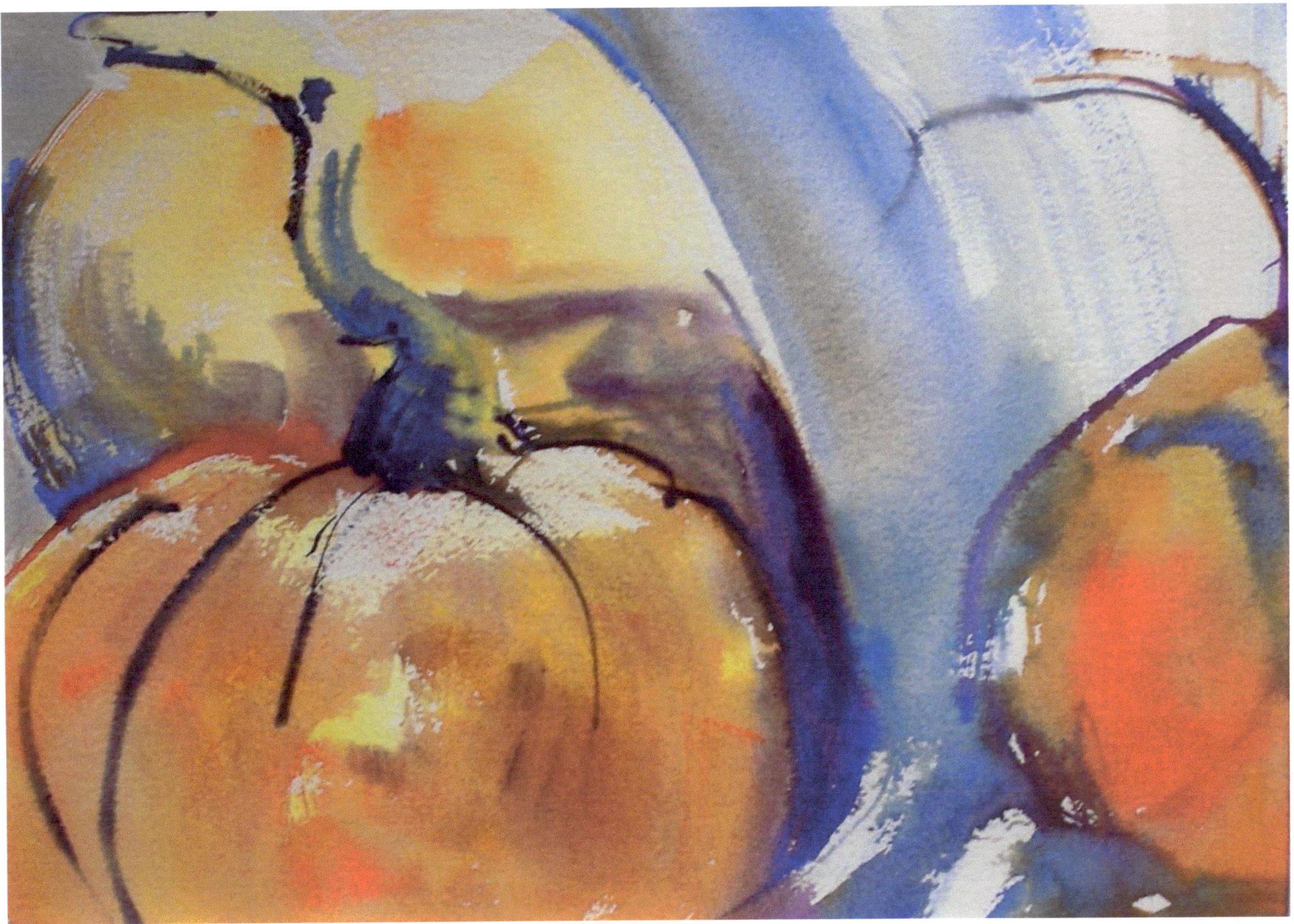

Pumpkins, no. 1, Watercolor, 14x10 in.

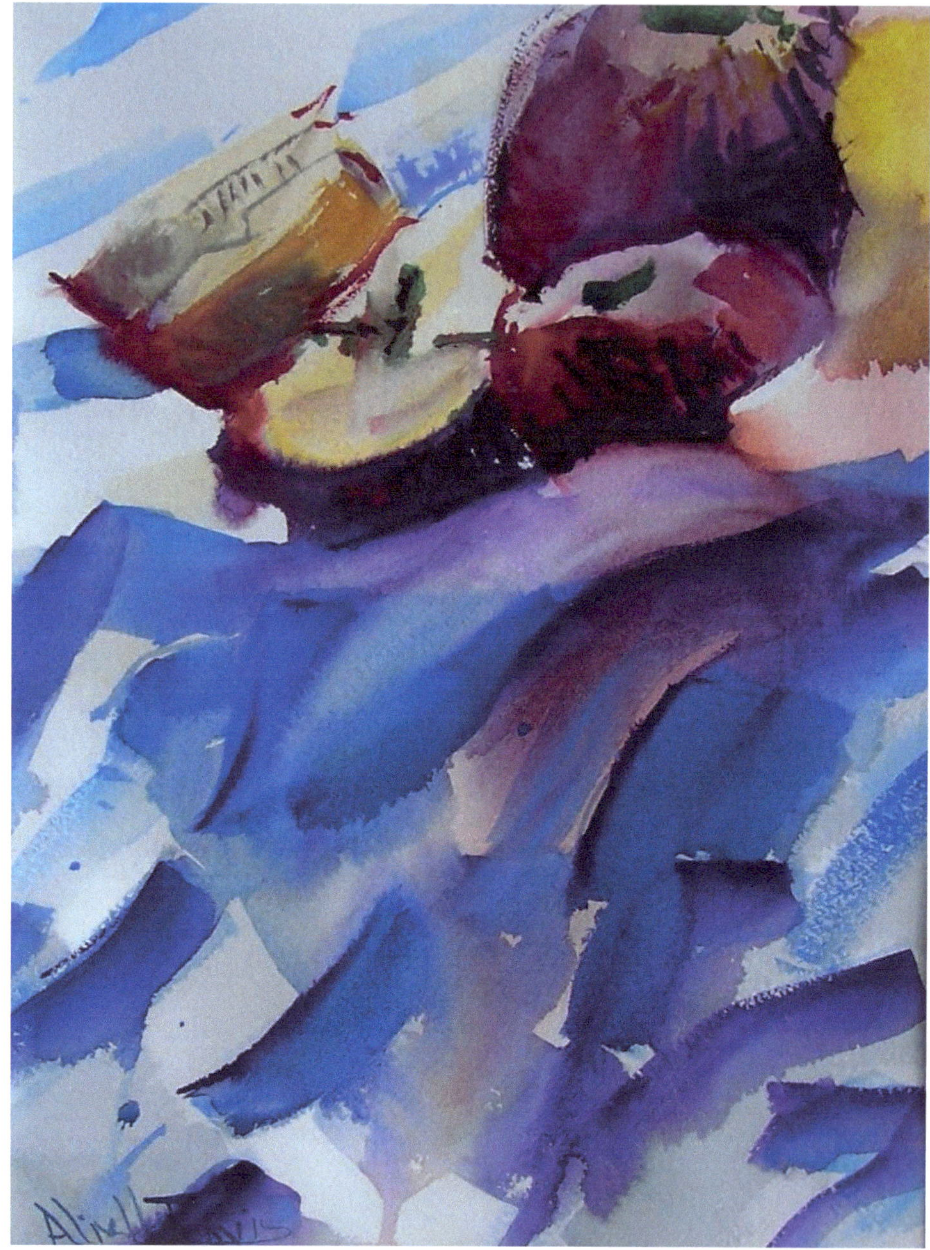

Apples on Blue Stripes, Watercolor, 10x14 in.

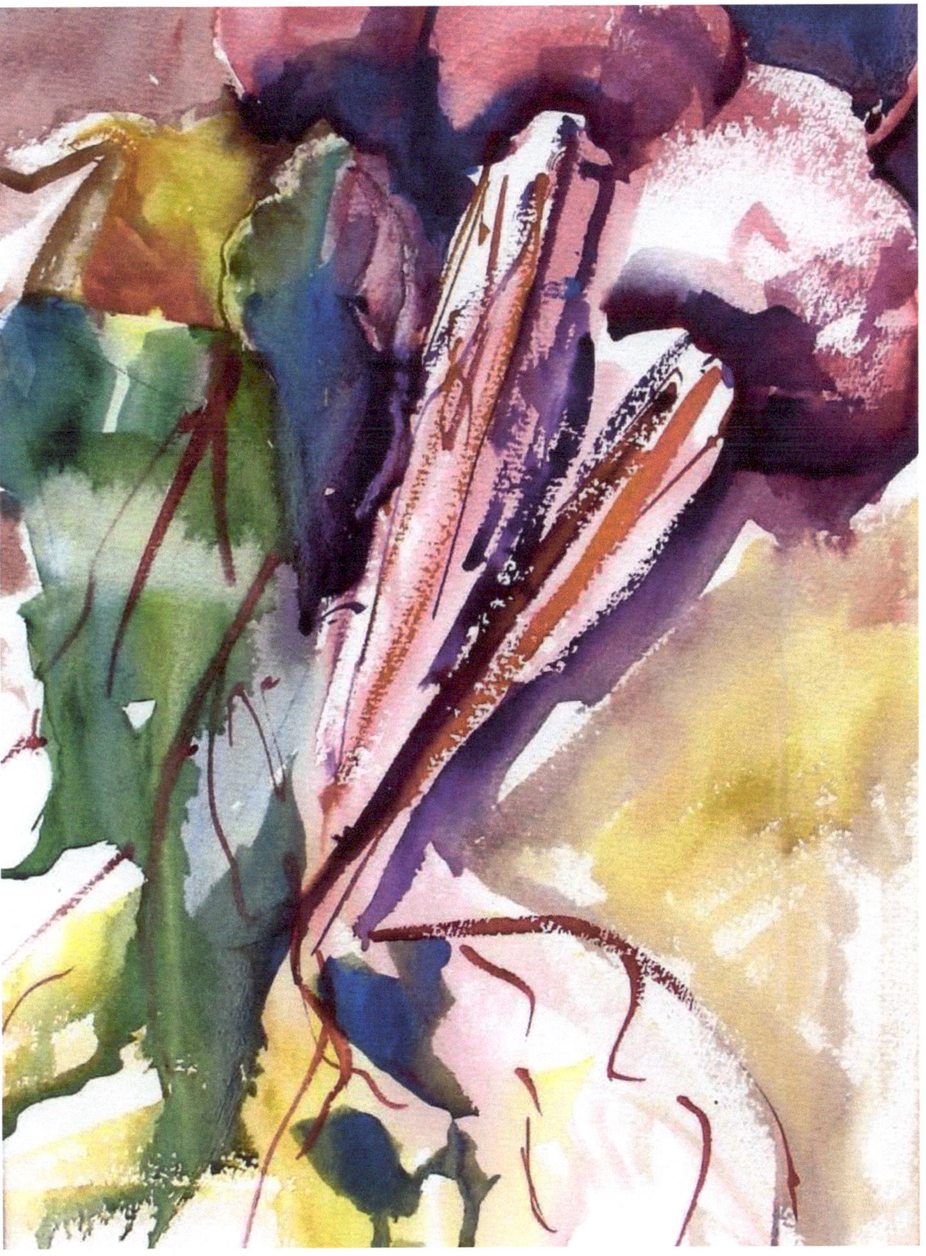

Beets, no. 2, Watercolor, 10x14 in.

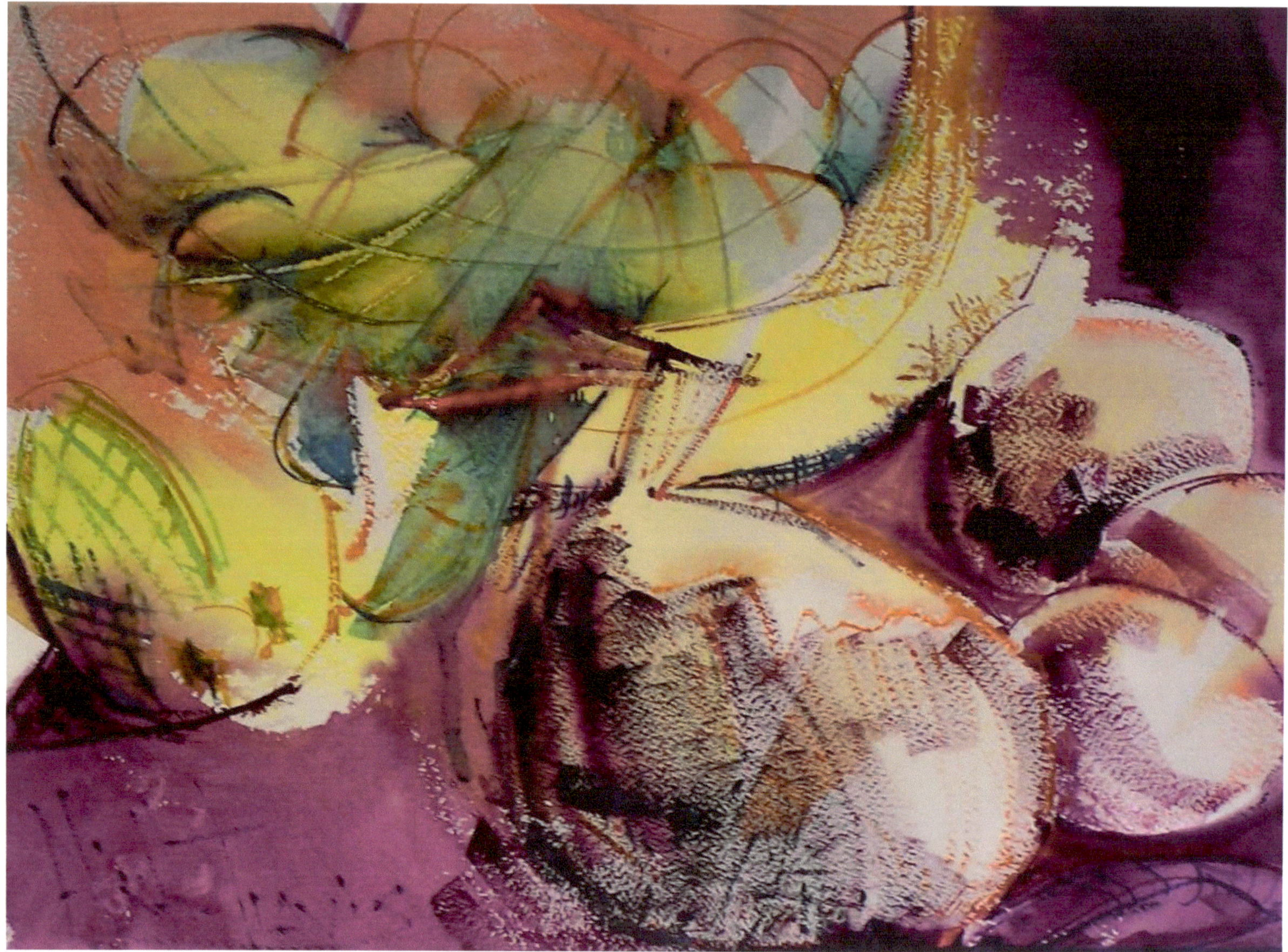

Potatoes with Onions, Watercolor, 14x10 in.

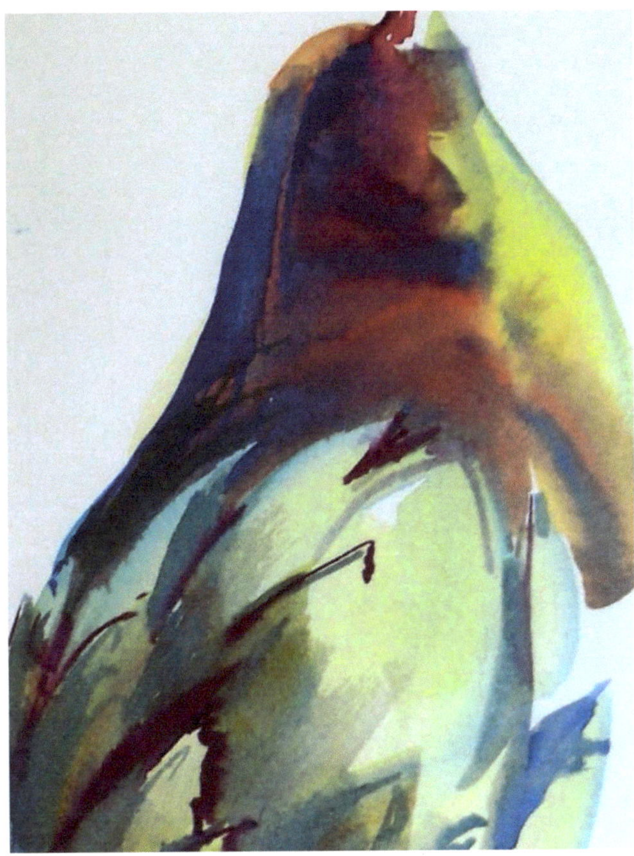

Artichoke with Pear, Watercolor, 4x6 in., *private collection*

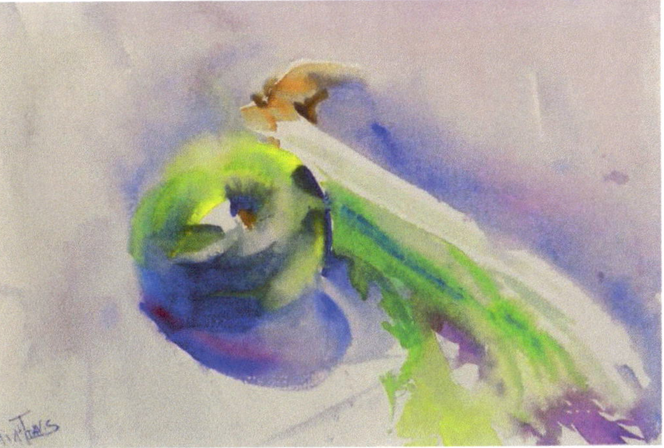

Apple with Celery, Watercolor, 7x6 in.

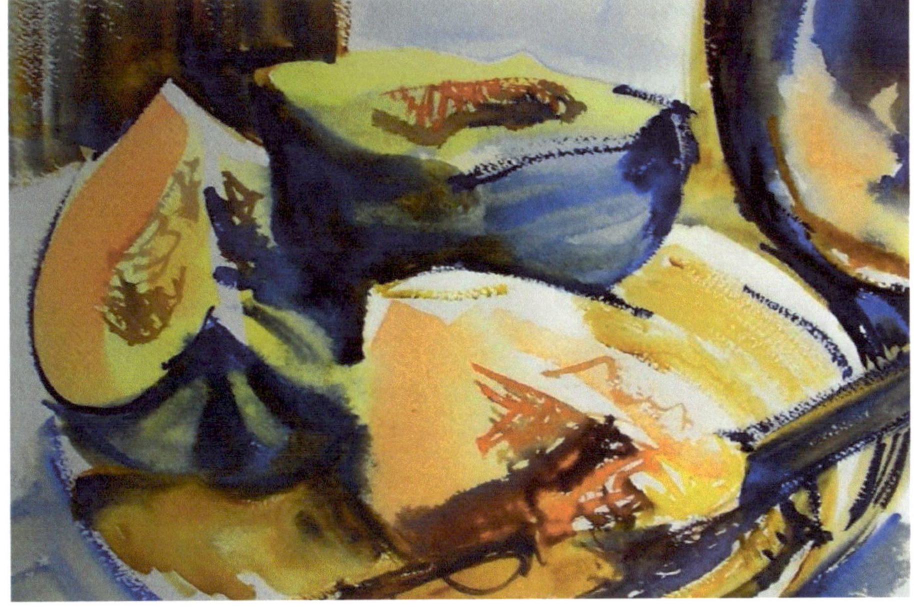

Sliced Acorn Squash with Reflection, Watercolor, 10x7 in.

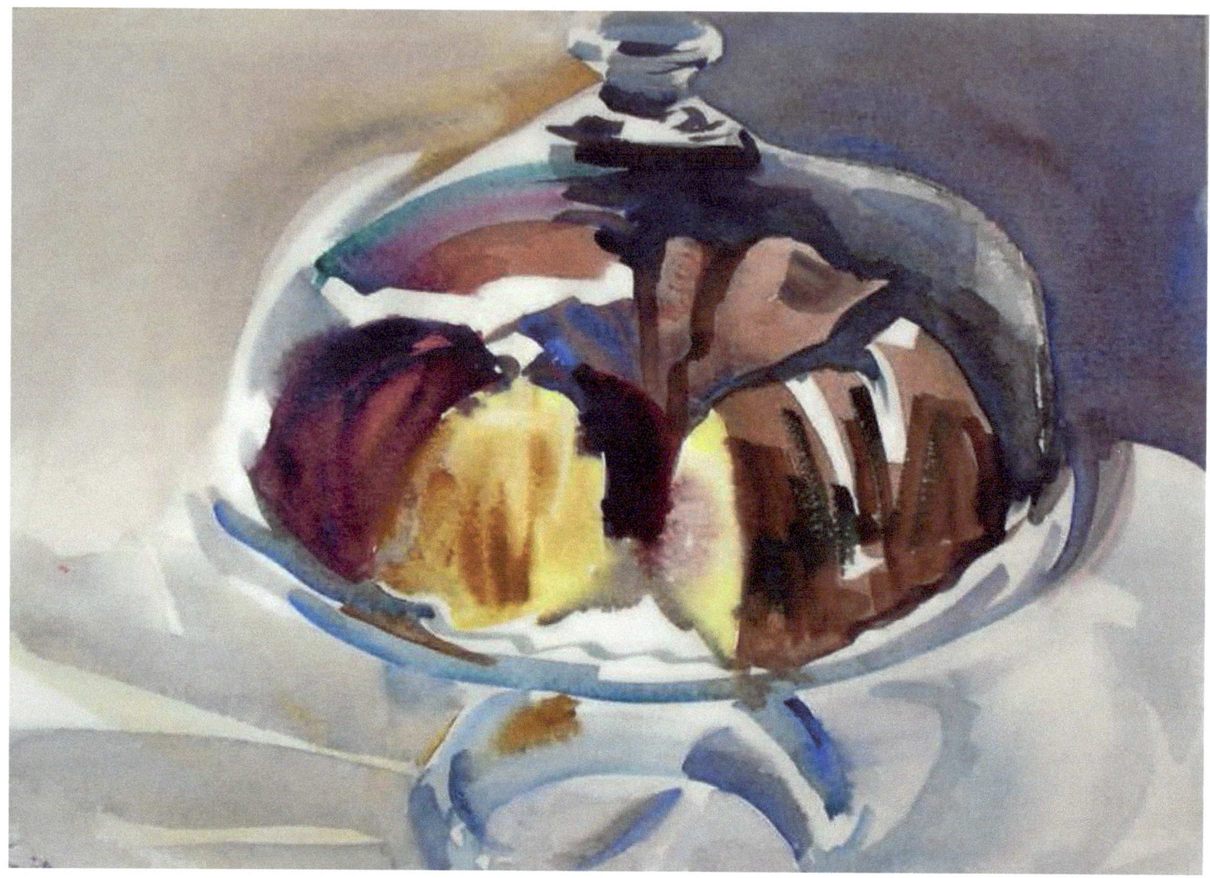

Fred's Birthday Cake, Watercolor, 14x10 in.

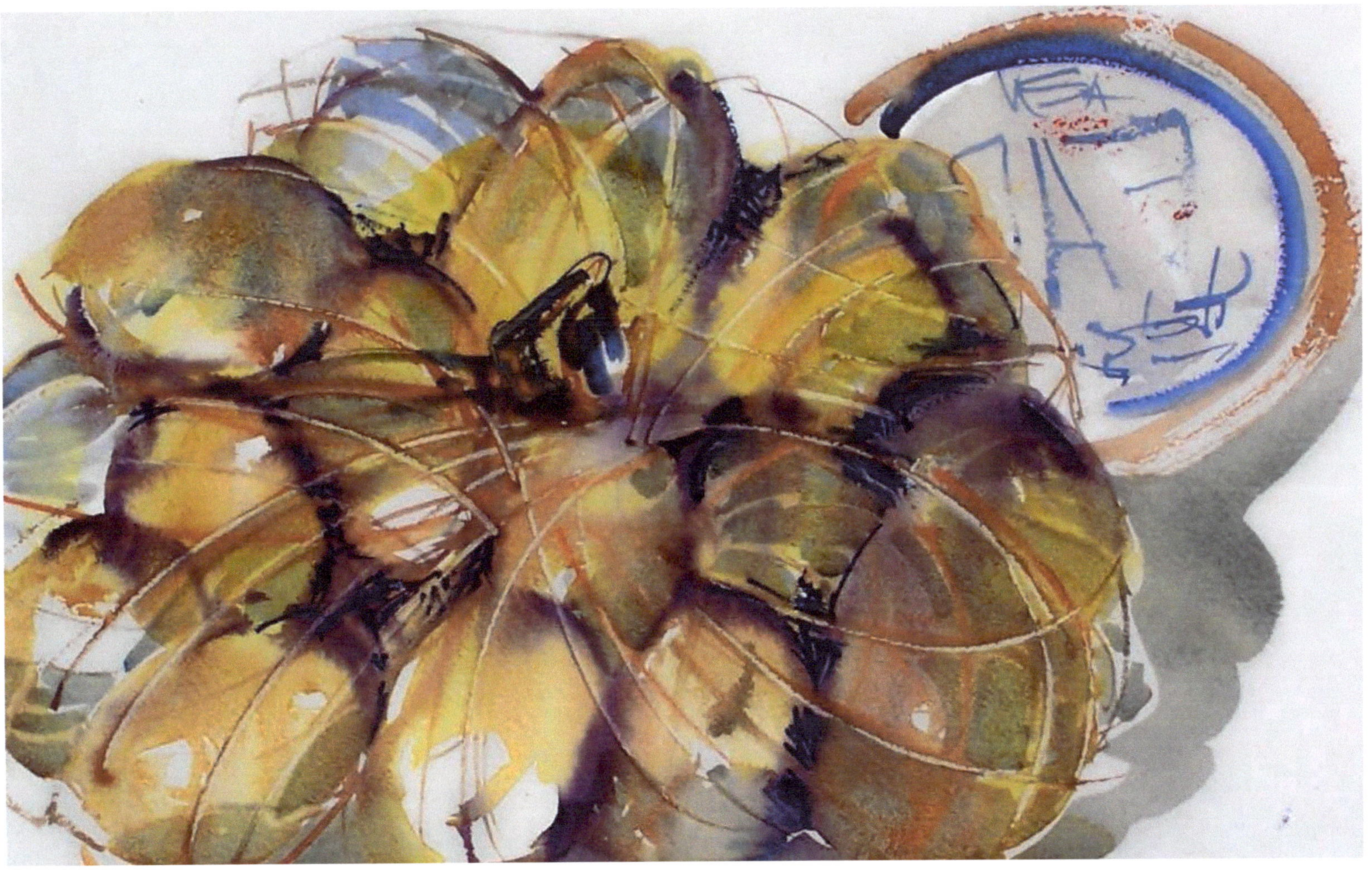

Bag of New Potatoes, Watercolor, 14x10 in.

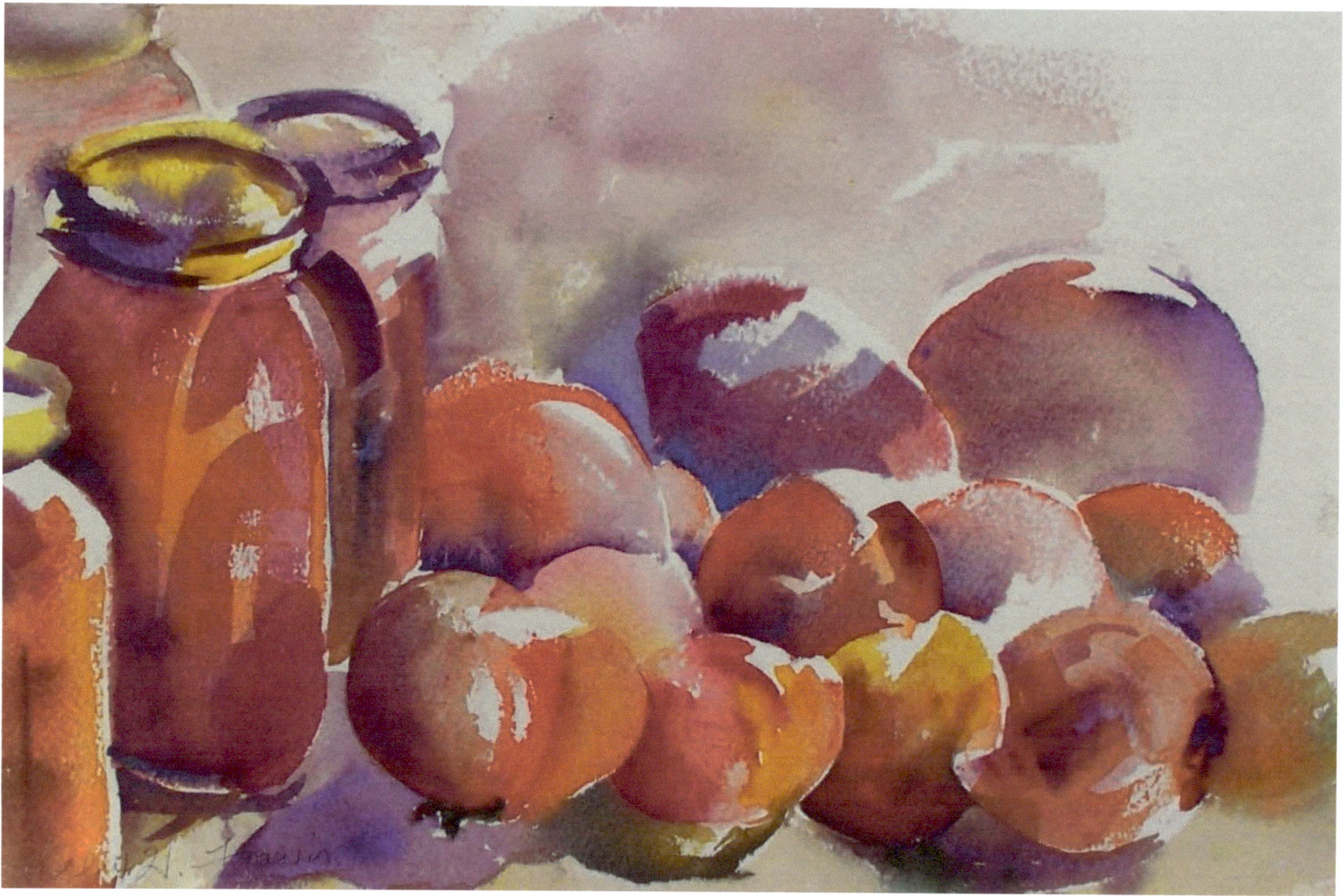

Fall Harvest, Watercolor, 14x10 in., *private collection*

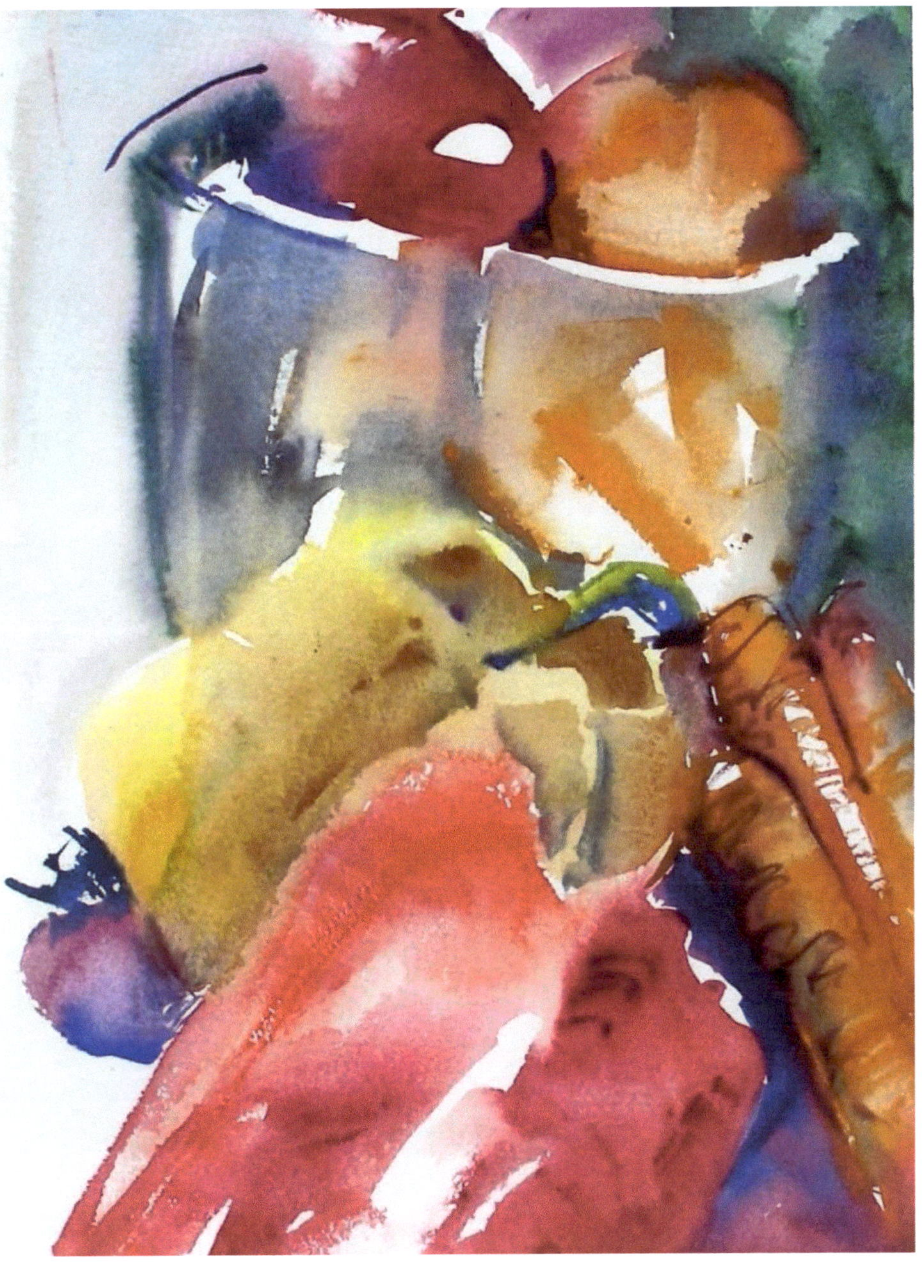

Peppers, Carrots with Reflection, Watercolor, 10x14 in.

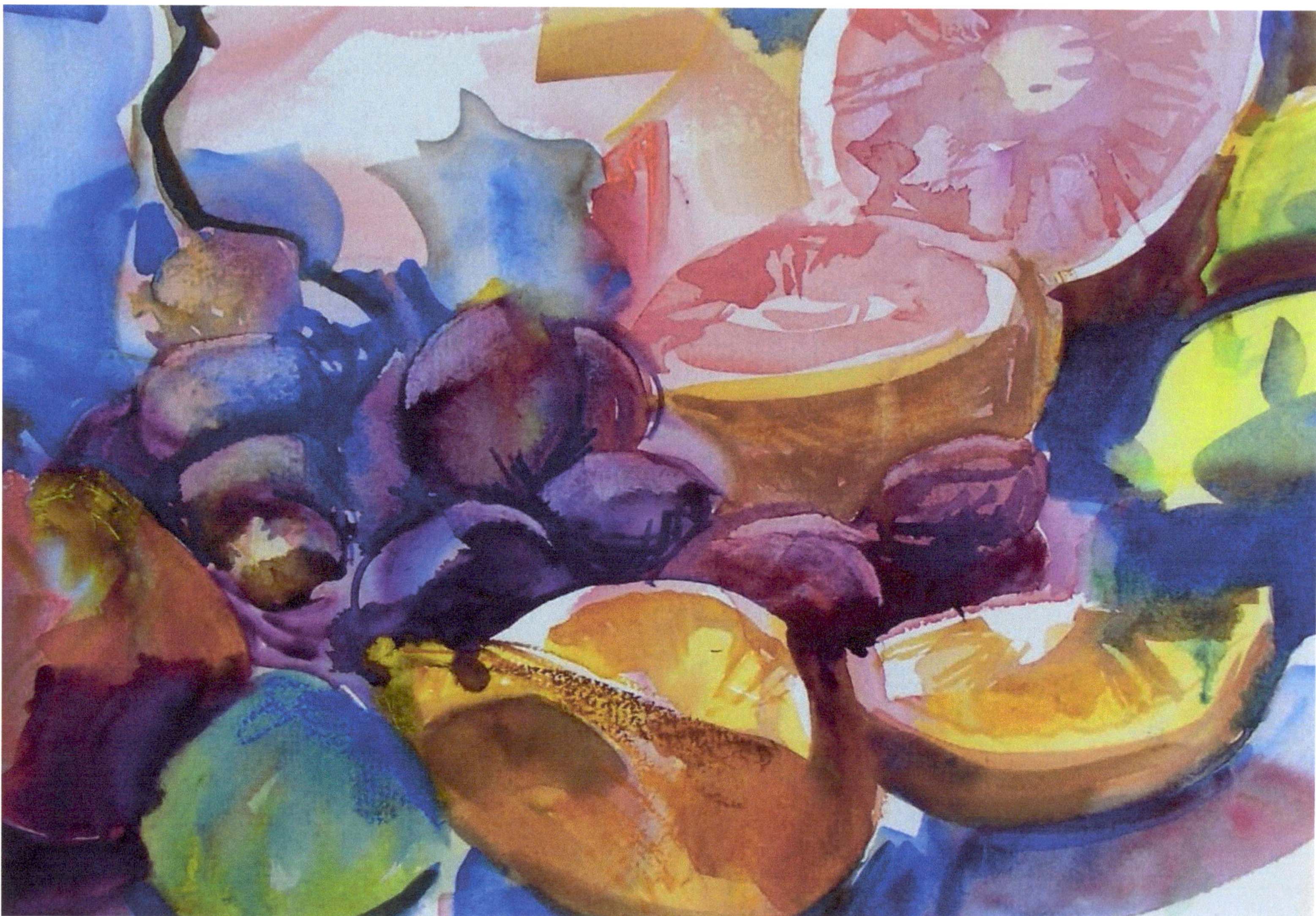

Cornucopia of Fruit, Watercolor, 14x10 in.

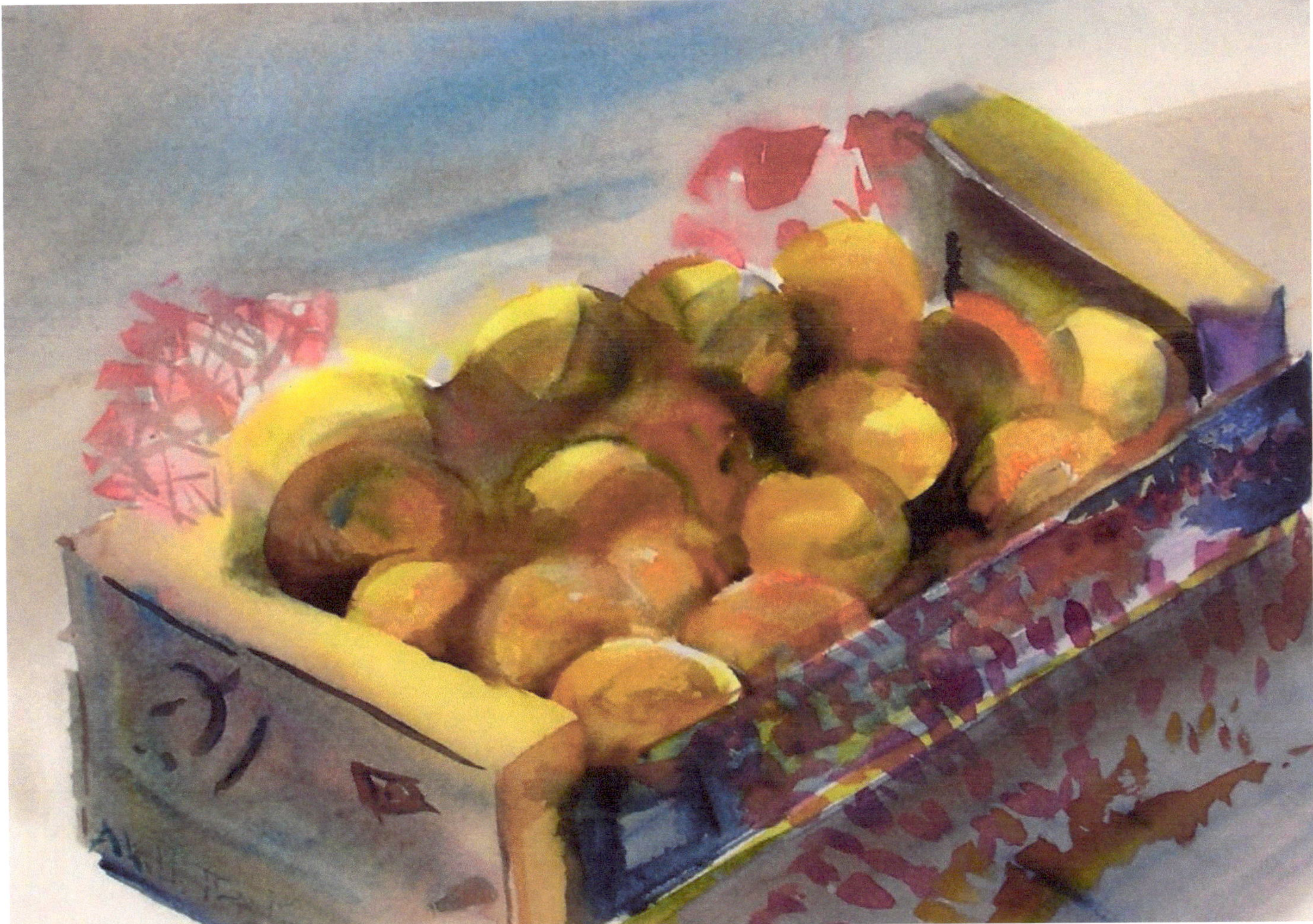

Holiday Clementines, Watercolor, 13x9 in.

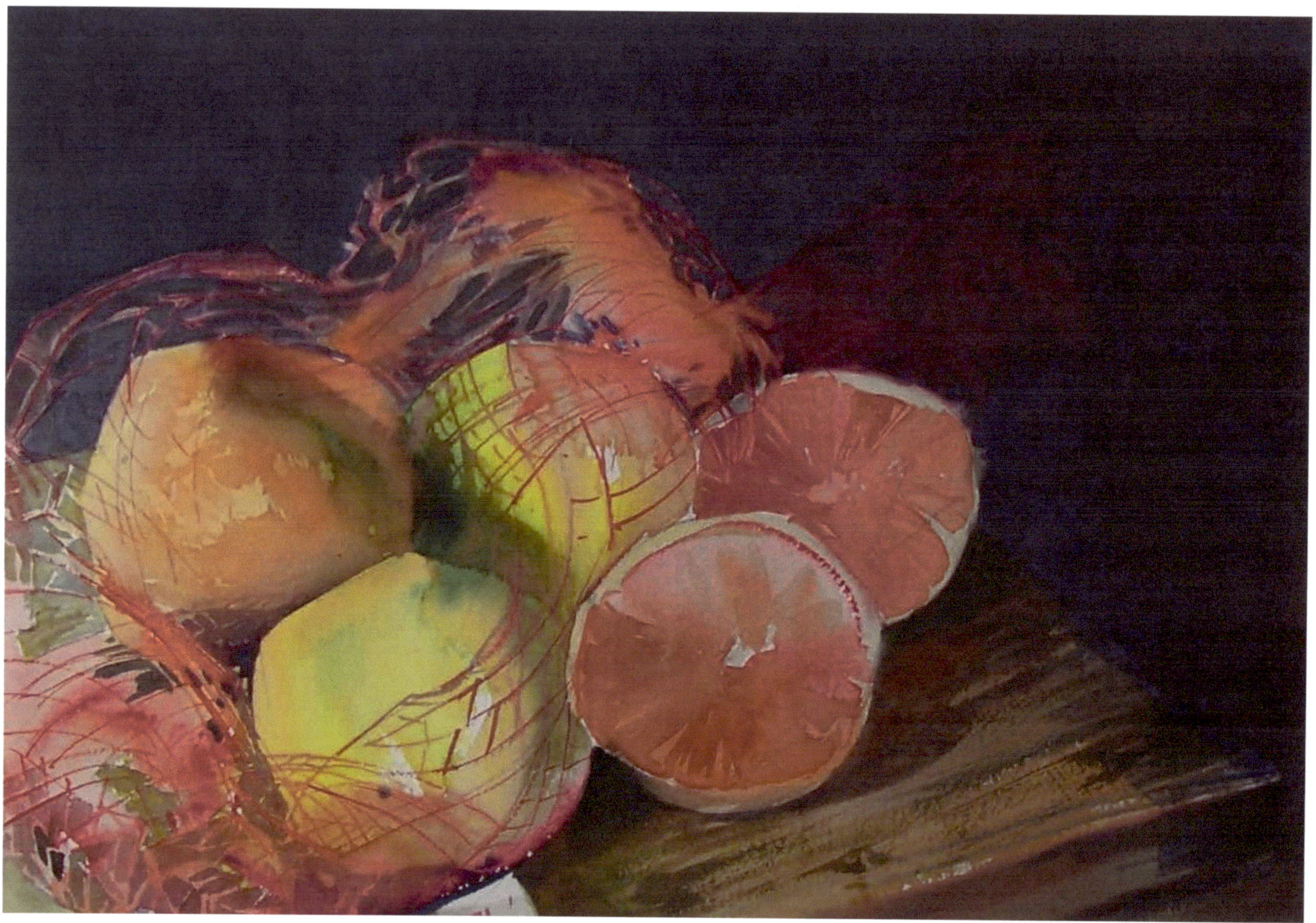

Bag of Grapefruit, Watercolor, 14x14 in.

Cake with Candles, Watercolor, 10x14 in.
"Honorable Mention", **Northeast Watercolor Society**, 2011